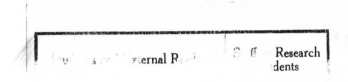

HISTORY
of
WESTERN
OIL SHALE

HISTORY
of
WESTERN
OIL SHALE

Paul L. Russell
Research Director, U.S. Bureau of Mines, 1967–1979

Edited by Arnold H. Pelofsky

DISTRIBUTED BY
APPLIED SCIENCE PUBLISHERS
LIMITED
Barking — Essex — England

THE CENTER FOR PROFESSIONAL ADVANCEMENT
EAST BRUNSWICK · NEW JERSEY

THE CENTER FOR PROFESSIONAL ADVANCEMENT
BOX H, EAST BRUNSWICK, NEW JERSEY 08816, USA

Publishing Consultant: Jack K. Burgess, Inc.

Library of Congress Cataloging in Publication Data
    Russell, Paul L.
      History of Western Oil Shale

      Bibliography: p.
      Includes Index.
      1. Oil-shales—The West—History. I. Pelofsky,
      Arnold H. II. Title.
      TN859. U52W477   553.2'82   80-66410
      ISBN 0-86563-000-3

Library of Congress Catalog Card Number 80-66410
International Standard Book Number 0-86563-000-3

Printed in the United States of America

To the memory of Dr. Charles H. Prien, who spent the last 35 years of his life on the problems of oil shale.

He is one of the Fathers of shale oil.

Table of Contents

PART I: EARLY HISTORY

PART II: 1915–1930

PART III: 1940–1969

PART IV: 1970–1979

PART V: SUMMARY AND EPILOGUE

List of Illustrations

List of Illustrations

Foreword

PAUL RUSSELL has compiled a comprehensive history of 65 years of western oil shale development. As an active oil shale research engineer for the past 35 years I can personally confirm the accuracy and completeness of his accounts of events in the three decades or more since World War II. These are the years which have seen the development of most of our present surface retorting processes, the initiation of on-site studies of in situ retorting, and the resumption of leasing of the federal oil shale lands.

The most fascinating part of this book is the early history of western oil shale from 1915 through 1930. This is the era of intensive filing of oil shale claims on the government lands, of financing and stock promotion schemes, and of the construction of mini-pilot plants. In this period there were eight "operating" plants in Colorado, five in Utah and two in Nevada, although total production from all of these was very small. As one reads of the financial difficulties and technical problems encountered, and relates them to present-day oil shale developments, one is impressed by the fact that there is little that is new "under the oil shale sun."

April, 1979   CHARLES H. PRIEN
Senior Research Fellow
Denver Research Institute
University of Denver

Preface

My first interest in oil shale began in 1948 when I was employed as a research mining engineer at the Bureau of Mines' oil shale mine near Rifle, Colorado. My employment covered the period during which most of the significant developments in oil shale mining and retorting were made. My interest in oil shale continued and in 1953 I investigated the Chattanooga Shales as a potential source of uranium and oil. As a result of my oil shale background I was later requested to serve as an expert witness in litigation involving the western oil shales. In preparation for this assignment, I not only read everything on the early history of western oil shales that I could lay my hands on, I also visited the sites of most of the early shale operations in Colorado. The first trip was made with Ralph Spengler, of the Bureau of Land Management, and germinated the first seed of an idea that I might some day attempt to collect most of the scattered information of these early operations into a single volume, along with as many photographs as could be found.

In 1967, I returned to Denver and continued to collect information and pictures of early oil shale activities. The proximity of Denver to many of the early shale activities and to collections of information on these activities provided the conditions for the decision that the time to prepare the long-planned book was at hand.

I hope that this book will help the reader to visualize and understand something of the history of those who have tried to develop this potentially vast energy source over a period of some 70 years. Success seems just around the corner again, as it often has in the past. Perhaps the next 70 years will result in a flourishing oil shale industry contributing to the energy requirements of these United States of America.

PAUL L. RUSSELL

Acknowledgments

PHOTOGRAPHY

A pictorial presentation of the early oil shale operations was a prime objective of this book. Many of the sites were visited and photographed by the author between the 1960s and the present. The need for photographs of the original installations was critical. Obtaining photographs of locations and events of the 1915–30 era presented substantial problems. Although photographs of the operations were taken and published, original negatives and prints now are rare. Most available early photographs are second or third generation copies of prints of published pictures. Quite often the quality and sharpness of the available print is less than desirable. However, sufficient detail remains to show the early operations.

Photography of the post-1944 era, although obtained from many sources, is of good quality.

Mr. Robert G. Shaw, professional photographer, Wheat Ridge, Colorado, provided the major portion of the photographic services and without his knowledge and assistance illustrating the text would have been even more difficult.

Source and credit for photographs are noted with each presentation.

ENCOURAGEMENT AND ASSISTANCE

The author gratefully acknowledges the encouragement and assistance given by the following people interested in oil shale, its history and its eventual use by the people of the United States:

John Donnell, Chief, Oil Shale Section, U.S. Geological Survey, Denver, Colorado;

Lowell Madsen, Solicitors Office, Department of the Interior, Denver, Colorado;

The late Dr. Charles H. Prien, University of Denver, Denver, Colorado;

Ralph Spengler, Mining Engineer, Bureau of Land Management, Denver, Colorado; and

Vern Whitham, Solicitors Office, Department of the Interior, Denver, Colorado.

To Arnold H. Pelofsky and Jack K. Burgess, the author expresses his appreciation of their diligence and care in the preparation of this book.

The author particularly wishes to thank his wife Florence, daughter Lillian, and son Roger, whose patience and help have been invaluable.

Introduction

"Only within the last few years have the American public, the Government and the American oil companies appreciated the gravity of the situation that will result from our oil supply becoming so depleted as to be inadequate to meet demands. The situation as regards petroleum is nowise different from that of any other natural resource. When the supply of any resource is plentiful and easily obtainable, little attention is paid to conservation or efficient utilization, but when the supply begins to fail, conservation begins to be applied and possible substitutes are sought."[1]

This sounds very familiar and could have been written at any time during the past few years. However, it is the opening paragraph used by Martin J. Gavin in Bulletin 210, *Oil Shale: An Historical, Technical, and Economic Study,* published in 1922. Gavin also stated: "As sources of substitutes for petroleum oils, the reserves of oil-shale in the United States stand out as most important."[2]

Interest in western oil shales began in about 1908, although the first retort to produce shale oil was not constructed until 1917 (the 1855 Mormon retort notwithstanding). Thus, the oil shales of the West have been considered of potential economic value for some 70 years. There have been periods of high interest, moderate interest, and no interest. Several hundred companies were formed, thousands of oil shale claims were located, stock was sold, and several retorts were constructed, a few of which actually produced oil.

Although the United States contains vast amounts of oil shale with an in-place oil content estimated as many times that of the known world reserves of petroleum, commercial production has eluded all efforts to date.

The term "oil shale" is a convenient expression used to cover a wide range of fine-grained sedimentary rocks most of which do not contain oil as such, but an organic matter derived mainly from aquatic organisms. The organic-rich matter frequently called kerogen may be converted to oil through destructive distillation.

Oil shale deposits are found in large areas of the United States (Fig 1) as well as in 14 foreign countries.

The oil shale deposits of the Green River Formation in Colorado, Utah and Wyoming (Fig 2), because of their size and grade, were considered as early as World War I to have the best potential for development. On the basis of today's knowledge, the Green River Formation represents the world's largest known single hydrocarbon resource. The approximately 17,000-square-mile area underlain by the formation is estimated to contain over 2000 billion

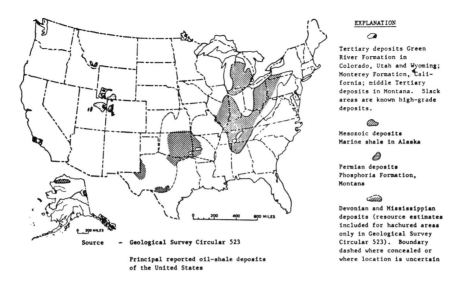

EXPLANATION

Tertiary deposits Green
River Formation in
Colorado, Utah and Wyoming;
Monterey Formation, Cali-
fornia; middle Tertiary
deposits in Montana. Black
areas are known high-grade
deposits.

Mesozoic deposits
Marine shale in Alaska

Permian deposits
Phosphoria Formation,
Montana

Devonian and Mississippian
deposits (resource estimates
included for hachured areas
only in Geological Survey
Circular 523). Boundary
dashed where concealed or
where location is uncertain

Source — Geological Survey Circular 523

Principal reported oil-shale deposits
of the United States

Fig. 1—Principal oil shale deposits of the United States. (From U.S. Geological Survey Circular 523.)

barrels of oil in place. The richest portion is in Colorado, where over one-half of the U.S. total resource lies.

Attempts to tap this vast resource occurred periodically from about 1915 to 1930, again from 1944 to date, and are continuing.

A great deal has been published about the past and the more current efforts to use our oil shale resources. Most of this information is widely scattered through technical journals, government reports, newspapers, treatises on petroleum and other publications. This book summarizes pertinent data of the published literature on the early and current efforts to commercialize the oil shales of the western United States. The so-called oil shales of California are not included since these deposits are for the most part not true oil shales, as most of the oil or bituminous material can be extracted by solvents. The oil shales of New Brunswick, Canada, are mentioned since there was an effort made to develop these shales during the same time period (1917–1930) that work was conducted on the western oil shales of the United States. The presentation is essentially non-technical and has as its primary purpose a one-document summation of the many attempts to produce oil from western oil shales.

PART I

EARLY HISTORY

Historical Notes

When and where the first oil was extracted from oil shale is not known. History does record that the word "petroleum" was used in England to describe such oil at least as early as the middle of the 14th century.[3] It is also of record that the first known oil shale patent, "A way to extract and make great quantityes of pitch tarr and oyle out of a sort of stone" was granted by British Crown Patent No. 330 in 1694.[4] History also records that the first commercial production began in France in 1838. The oil shale industry of Scotland, which dates back to 1850, grew to much larger proportions than that in France and survived for more than a century. The Scottish industry, which may well have been the most successful commercial operation to date, produced fuels, chemicals and waxes until operations stopped in 1964.

Between 1850 and 1950, oil was produced from oil shales at various times in Australia, Estonia (U.S.S.R.), Germany, Manchuria (China), Spain, South Africa and Sweden.[5] All of these oil shale operations were supported by Government subsidies of some sort, and all except those in the U.S.S.R. and China failed because of inability to compete with natural petroleum. It is believed that the U.S.S.R. and China operations could not, and would not, have been operated without subsidies.

The earliest record found by the author of oil shale investigation in North America is that of Dr. Abram Gasner, who erected a small retort at Baltimore, New Brunswick, Canada, in 1815 for the purpose of treating Albertite shales found there.[6]

A small oil shale industry developed in Canada and the Eastern United States, and by 1860 more than 50 companies were producing oil by distillation of various kinds of bituminous substances. The methods used were crude, and the materials treated ranged from bituminous and cannel coals to some oil shales. The product was kerosene or "coal oil". Many of these companies were just getting started when petroleum became plentiful owing to developments that followed the Drake discovery of an oil well in Pennsylvania in 1859. With plentiful petroleum, the shale oil operations became unprofitable and either were converted to use the new oil from wells or were abandoned.[7]

As petroleum supplies increased, interest in oil shales decreased, and published evidence of oil shale activity was very limited until the early 1900s when recognition of western oil shales started a new era of interest. This interest in western oil shale accelerated with the petroleum shortages prior to and during World War I. Those post-World War I activities in western shales instigated the preparation of this document. In documenting such history, however, it appeared logical to include the events following World War II when potential petroleum shortages caused another resurgence of interest in western oil shales that is continuing as this is being written.

GREEN RIVER AND NEVADA OIL SHALES

The Green River oil shales were deposited during the Eocene Geologic Epoch some 50 million years ago in two large lakes: Lake Uinta that covered what is now the Uinta and Piceance Creek Basins and Lake Gosiute that covered what is now the present Green River and Washakie Basins (Fig 2). After depositions, the region was warped into several structural basins and later elevated several thousand feet above sea level. Subsequent erosion of the structurally high areas has exposed the oil shale in a series of cliffs and ledges around the edge of the basins.

About 80 percent of the potential oil shale resource of the Green River Formation, or about 1200 billion barrels of oil equivalent, lies in the Piceance Creek Basin of Colorado. Of this total, about 480 billion barrels are contained in shales averaging 25 or more gallons of oil per ton. The higher grade shale sections range from 10 to more than 2000 feet in thickness and may be covered with overburden ranging from 0 to more than 1500 feet. In Utah the rich oil shale is restricted to a single section known as the Mahogany Zone which may be 50 or more feet in thickness and average about 25 gallons of oil per ton. Oil shales of Wyoming tend to be thin and of only moderate richness.

The oil shales of Nevada occur mostly in the eastern area near Elko and Carlin and like the Green River Formation are Tertiary in age. The beds are rather thin, dip steeply, and are extensively folded and faulted. The richest seam is about four feet thick and yields 28 gallons of oil to the ton.

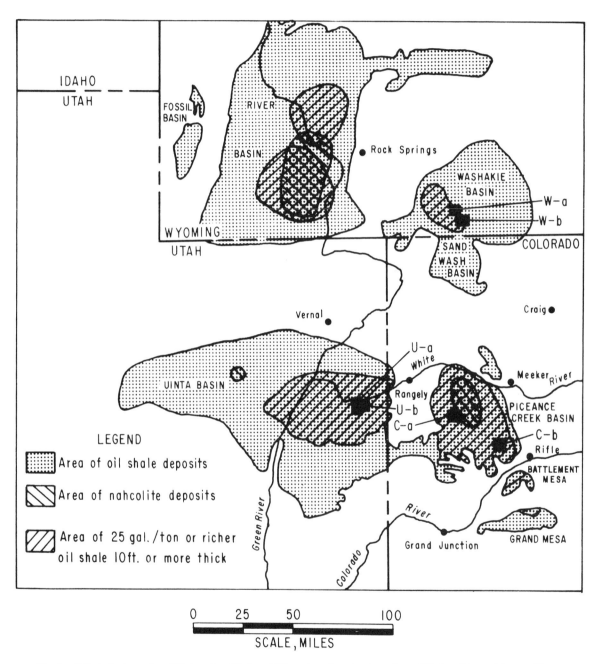

Fig. 2—*Oil shale deposits of Colorado, Utah and Wyoming showing location of Federal Lease Tracts. (From U.S. Bureau of Mines.)*

Early Activity in Western Shales

"The Rock that Burns" was an Indian name for oil shale indicating early recognition that this was an unusual material. The story, true or not, of a fireplace constructed by an early settler of a "pretty" rock which burned and destroyed the building on its first use, is also recognition of a sort. Better evidence of recognition is the ruins of an old retort on a tributary of Chriss Creek, Juab County, Utah, believed to have been used by the Mormons to distill oil from oil shale prior to 1859. It is believed the product was used as a dressing for harnesses and other leather goods, as a lubricant (axle grease) and as a fuel in crude lamps.

In Colorado, Roane Rowley and T. E. Bailey are reported to have experimented with shale as a smudge for Palisade peach orchards some time prior to 1905. James Doyle, discoverer and developer of the famous Portland gold mine at Cripple Creek, Colorado, entered the Mount Logan and Parachute Creek areas in about 1908 and is credited as having been the first to propose recovering commercial oil from oil shales. Doyle, with the assistance of C. A. Fisher, a midwest geologist, J. C. Sparks, a New York chemist, and Ralph Arnold, is credited with bringing the immense deposits of bituminous rock in Colorado and Utah to the attention of the United States Government.[8] This awareness led Woodruff and Day of the U.S. Geological Survey to conduct field studies starting in 1913 and to publish Bulletin 581 in 1914. The U.S. Bureau of Mines also published a Bulletin on oil shales in 1914, and Dean E. Winchester of the Geological Survey began his examination of oil shales in 1915. These studies, in turn, resulted in President Wilson establishing a 45,444 acre Naval Oil Shale Reserve in Colorado and an 86,584 acre Naval Oil Shale Reserve in Utah, in December 1916. President Coolidge added 23,000 acres to the Colorado Reserve and 4,880 acres to the Utah Reserve in 1924. James Doyle and Joseph Bellis located mining claims under the 1872 Mining Law in about 1911 and were among the first to do so.[9]

THE GREAT LAND RUSH

Dean Winchester's first examination of the oil shales in about 1915 indicated a potential recovery of 20 billion barrels of oil, or three times the then estimated national petroleum reserve. An early recheck was ordered; but more detailed sampling merely increased it by 100 percent, or to 40 billion barrels of oil. The results of his work were published in 1917 by the U.S. Geological Survey.

The 1917 annual report of Secretary of the Interior, Franklin K. Lane, stated: "As a result of the investigation of the western oil shales, it is believed that it is now commercially feasible to work selected deposits of shale in competition with the oil from oil wells, and that these oil-shale reserves can be considered of immediate importance to the oil industry and to the defence of the nation." This report along with the glowing article, "Billions of Barrels Locked up in Rocks", published in 1918 by the National Geographic Magazine, was widely circulated and quoted in the magazines and newspapers of the day. Both the publicity and an increasing demand for liquid fuels instigated a stampede to locate oil shale claims that was similar to the earlier gold and silver rushes so familiar to Colorado and the West.

The Oil Placer Act of 1872 authorized citizens of the United States to locate, by legal subdivision, land valuable for oil shale in tracts not to exceed 160 acres each by using names of eight bonafide locators on each 160 acre section, or one name for each 20 acres, or fractional part thereof. It is estimated that as many as 10 thousand claims in Colorado, with an additional 25–27 thousand claims in Utah and Wyoming, may have been filed before the Oil Placer Act was replaced by the 1920 Minerals Leasing Act. The 1920 Act prevented further filing of mining claims and provided that publicly-owned shale lands could be leased only by the Secretary of the Interior. By February 25, 1920, when President Wilson signed the Leasing Act, virtually every available acre of cliff outcrops had been claimed in Colorado, Utah and Wyoming.[10] There was no knowledge of the rich, deep, basin center in Colorado and claims were not filed in this area.

The Leasing Act of 1920 did little to slow activities in oil shale. By 1922 at least 100 oil shale corporations had been founded and possibly another 150 were added before the end of the boom in 1930.[11] Additionally, on May 12, 1920, the Department of the Interior ruled that oil shale lands upon which title had been properly initiated prior to the passage on February 25, 1920, of the Oil Leasing Bill, may be passed to patent under the Oil Placer Act. This announcement that oil shale lands could be taken to patent was joyfully received, and it led to considerable activity in surveying and consolidating claims and performing the annual $100 per-year per-claim assessment work required by law. One estimate was that: "A million dollars is being spent this season [1920] toward securing of patents based upon an estimated 10,000 claims in the Grand Valley–De Beque area since each required $100 worth of work."[12] Many sales and exchanges of acreage occurred. Prospective purchasers were advised to take particular care to ascertain that the title to land was clear because numerous cases of claim-jumping and fraudulent entry were reported in Colorado and Utah.[13] Land titles often were clouded and ownership was in dispute. The local land office also warned that all titles would be thoroughly investigated and that dummy locations were invalid.

ASSESSMENT WORK

Table I lists assessment work reported by the Colorado Bureau of Mines for the years 1920 through 1923. Table II lists the principal oil shale land holders in Colorado as of 1928.

The success of the patent effort is indicated by records of the United States Land Office at Glenwood Springs, which shows that on November 10, 1922, in the oil shale area of Colorado, 25,901.82 acres of oil shale land had been patented. In addition, final certificates had been issued for 15,887.88 acres and applications pending aggregated 6,850.80 acres more. The largest holders were the Colorado Carbon Company and the Ventura Consolidated Oil Fields Company at De Beque and the Union Oil Company at Grand Valley. The Union Oil Company alone had patented 16,011.16 acres and action on an additional 4000 acres was in progress.[14] Patent action also was taking place in Utah and Wyoming, but at a slower pace.

Few mining claims as such were filed in what is now the center of the Piceance Creek Basin. However, the presence of water in Piceance Creek and its tributaries attracted farmers and ranchers, and homesteads soon covered most land in the valley bottoms. The homesteads eventually were "proved-up" and became private land.

Figure 3 shows the 1977 ownership of oil shale lands in Colorado and Utah.

TABLE I

THE COLORADO BUREAU OF MINES' REPORTS FOR THE YEARS 1920, 1921, 1922, 1923, AND 1924 SHOWING THAT ASSESSMENT WORK WAS CLAIMED BY THE FOLLOWING COMPANIES FOR ONE OR MORE OF THESE YEARS.

Name	*Location*
Alturus Shale Co., & American Keroleum Co.	Both were P. C. Coryell & Co. holdings in Garfield County
American Mineral Oil Co.	Parachute Creek
American Shale Refining Company	Roan Creek
T. E. Bailey & Co.	Parachute Creek
Bailes & Carlisle Holdings	Carr, Roan & Brush Creeks
T. W. Bell Holdings	Near Grand Valley
Battlement Mesa Oil Shale Co.	Battlement Mesa
The Belvedere Oil Shale and Refining Company	Dry Fork
Black Prince Shale Co.	30 miles from Fruita
Black Queen Shale Co.	Dry Fork
Brush Creek Oil Shale Co.	Collbran
Brumstead Holdings	Brush & Roan Creeks
Callahan Holdings & Callahan Oil Shale Co.	Parachute Creek
Campbell Refining Corp.	Clear Creek
Champion Oil Shale and Refining Company	West of Rifle
Colorado Oil Shale Co.	Battlement Mesa
Colorado Carbon Company	Kimball Creek
Columbia Oil Shale Refining Co.	E. Fork Parachute Creek

TABLE I—*continued*

Name	Location
Continental Oil Shale Mining and Refining Company	Piceance Creek
De Beque Shale Oil Co.	Between Brush & Roan Creeks
Doyle (Reed) Holdings	Not noted
Eaton Holdings	Parachute Creek
Felton, L. M. Jr., Option	Not noted
Gary Oil Shale Holdings	E. Middle Fork Parachute Creek
Girard Holdings	Near De Beque
The Grand Valley Oil & Shale Co.	Starkey Gulch
Gregory, J. E., Holdings	Not noted
Hendrick Placers	T.6 R.96 W
Hub Oil Shale Producing and Refining Co.	Not noted
Indoxoline Plant	Mt. Blaine
Index Oil Shale Co.	Roan Creek
Jones Group	Between Parachute & Roan Creeks
Leadville Shale Oil & Refining Co.	Not noted
Little Jim Claims	Parachute Creek
Lyons, L. P. Holdings	Clear Creek
The March Oil Shale Co.	Wheeler Gulch
McMullen (Samuel) Holdings	Kimball Creek
Mt. Blair Oil Shale Co.	Mt. Blaine
Mt. Mann Group	Mt. Mann
The Monarch Oil Shale Company	Conn Creek
Mt. Logan Mine	Mt. Logan
Mountain Boy & Annex	Not noted
Nelson, Emil J. Holdings	Not noted
Ochner Holding Co.	Battlement Mesa
Overland Shale Co.	Dry Fork
Pilot Oil Shale Mining Co.	Grand Valley
Phenol Group	Between Roan & Carr Creeks
Pyramid Shale Co.	Near Collbran
Rulison Plant (U.S.B.M.)	6 miles from Rulison
The Searchlight Oil Shale & Refining Company	Clear Creek
Shale Oil Syndicate	Not noted
S.O.S. & Lucky Strike Group	Not noted
Sterling Oil Co.	Dry Fork
Sullivan D. A. Claims	Not noted
Superior Shale Oil Co.	Long Point
Taff, G. A. Agent	Wheeler Gulch
Uintah Basin Products & Development Co.	Parachute Creek
Ute Rock Group	Kimball Creek
Ventura Consolidated Oil Fields Co.	Brush & Roan Creeks
Virginia Colorado Development Co.	Battlement Mesa
Wanita Oil Shale Co.	Not noted
Washington Shale Oil & Product Company	Conn Creek

TABLE II

PRINCIPAL OIL SHALE LAND HOLDERS IN COLORADO AS OF 1928

Owner	Acres (approximate)	Owner	Acres (approximate)
Naval Reserve	60,000	Eaton Investment Co.	8,500
*Crystal Shale Oil Corp.	20,000	Continental Oil Shale Mining and Refining Company	8,000
Paraire Oil & Gas Co.	19,500	American Shale Refining Co.	6,500
Union Oil Co. of California, Inc.	19,000	Standard Oil Company of New Jersey	6,300
Columbia Oil Shale and Refining Company (Gregory Wheeler Holdings)	14,400	Karl Schuyler and Associates	6,000
Honolulu Oil Co.	13,000	General Shale Corporation	4,000
Verner Z. Reed Estate	9,000	Shaffer Oil & Refining Co.	3,700
Columbia Oil Shale and Refining Company	8,600	Other Miscellaneous	18,500
		TOTAL	225,000

Became property of Getty Oil Company

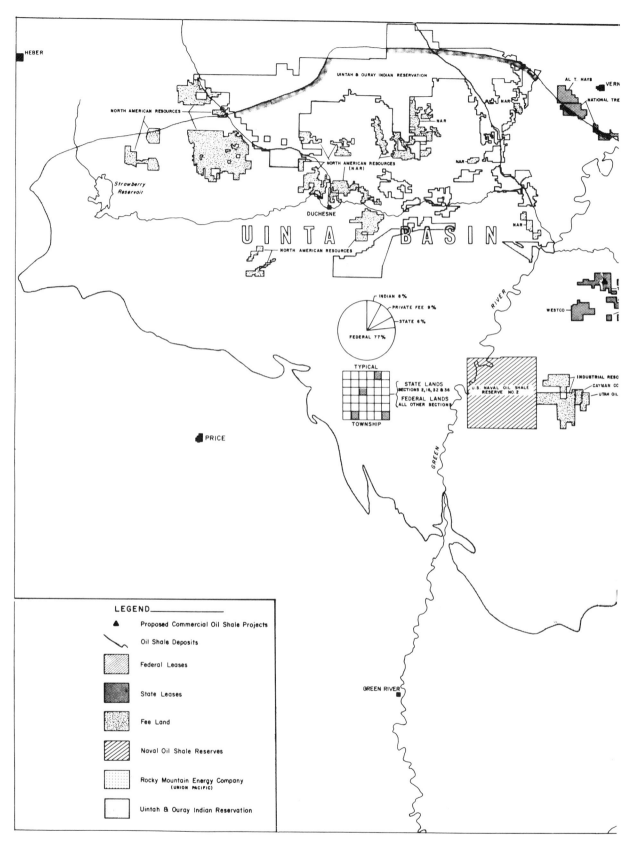

Fig. 3—(a) and (b): Adapted from 1977 land ownership map compiled by and courtesy of The Pace Company Consultants and Engineers, Inc. (formerly Cameron Engineers).

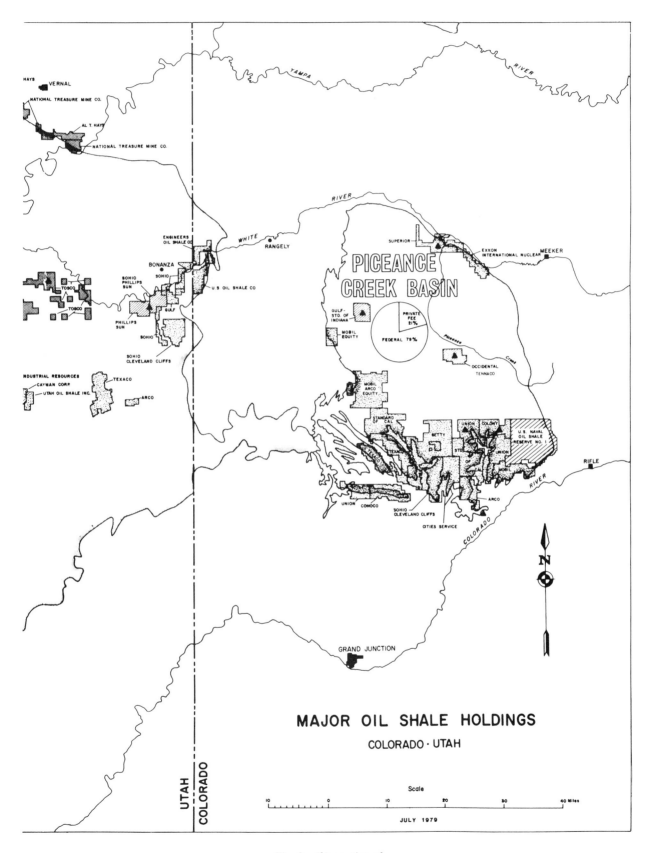

Fig. 3—(b) continued.

The homestead law at that time included mineral rights with the land, and the homesteaders thus became owners of some of the choice oil shale mineral rights in the Piceance Creek Basin. However, these homesteads covered only a small portion of the basin. Their relatively small size, together with some 500–1500 ft. depths of overburden between their surface and the higher grade shale beds, did not make them attractive mining sites. Land adjacent to the homesteads was and is for the most part Public Lands controlled by the U.S. Government. Private industrial interests now control most of the original homesteads although in many cases they continue to be operated as ranches by their former owners under lease-back arrangements. Such arrangements provide industry with a foothold in the Basin and land for trading and/or negotiation with the Government to "block-up" or consolidate adjacent lands of sufficient area and shale resource to support future mining operations.

The question of validity of oil shale claims has been in and out of the U.S. Courts for many years. Many patents have been issued since the 1920s, but only a few since the 1960s. The Government has contested most recent patent attempts. The questions of claim validity, assessment work and other items continue to be litigated today, case by case, with no indication of a broad solution.

FINANCING
AND STOCK PROMOTIONS

The oil shale boom of 1915–1930 was born during a period when there was reason to believe that shale oil soon would be needed to replace or supplement decreasing supplies of well petroleum. However, the prominent feature of the oil shale boom might be described as over-promotion, and much of it fraudulent.

The rush to obtain oil shale lands was the first action. Once oil shale claims were obtained, the holder had an option of selling, developing, or simply holding the claims for future speculation or development. For the latter, he needed to do assessment work aggregating $100 per claim, per year, possibly leading to a patent. Development or holding required funds, something most of the claim holders did not have in abundance. Sale of stock was an established method of raising funds for mining and other development, and this course quickly was taken by many. Gavin[15] described this era as follows:

"Many operators and organizers worked in good

faith, but the potential industry was adversely affected by the fake promoter and his promotion companies. Many promotions had a single objective—fattening the pocketbooks of the promoters—and some were quite successful in doing this. The situation for the shady operator was near ideal, the years 1918–20 were possibly the height of a speculative era. Many people had made their first investment by purchasing Government bonds or similar secure items. Most were unable to differentiate between an investment and a speculation so were ripe for [fast] operators who easily convinced them that their present investments should be changed into ones yielding a higher return. The country was literally 'wild over oil.' In the popular imagination, anything connected with oil was a source of immediate wealth, and stock promoters dealing in oil shale stock did not hesitate to make the prospects more dazzling by presenting all sorts of impossible estimates of assured profits in oil shale ventures."

The estimate by the Government of "billions of barrels" of oil in western oil shales was used to good advantage. One sales promotion consisted of erecting model retorts in booths on State Street in Chicago and on Larimer Street in Denver. Stock certificates were sold to passers-by who were assured the billowing clouds of black smoke from the model retort represented pure oil and that there was a lot more where that came from. Other promotional activities consisted of on-site tours of construction activities, including observation of retorts in operation. In many cases, the retort was started-up on the morning of the demonstration and was closed down as soon as the tour group left. In some instances, it appeared that tar sands may have been used for the demonstration rather than oil shale because the retorts apparently worked better with this material. Figure 4 shows one such announcement of oil shale demonstrations at which it is assumed that stock was available for purchase.

The need for capital for successful shale oil development was recognized by many as shown by the following:

"It should be borne in mind that the oil shale industry is not a 'poor-man's game' in the sense that a small amount of capital invested .will bring fabulous returns. On the contrary, it is distinctly a 'rich man's game' in the sense that a large amount of capital must be invested before there is any return whatever."[16]

The DeBeque Chamber of Commerce

Invites You to DeBeque to Make a Trip at Their Expense Through the Shale Fields, October Third

All Visitors Will Be Served With

Barbecued Venison and Free Lunch

Special train with reduced rates leaves Denver 3:55 p. m. Saturday, October 2nd ,arriving at DeBeque at 8:15 a. m. Sunday

Visit DeBeque the Oil Shale Center

Seven creeks converging at De-Beque, Colorado, show over 200 miles of shale escarpment.

Fig. 4—Announcement of oil shale demonstrations near De Beque, Colorado. (From The Mountain States Mineral Age, *Spring, 1920.)*

and ". . . but, also, ample capital must be provided for proper development and expensive equipment. . . . The mining or business man with limited capital at its [his] disposal cannot hope to engage in the exploitation of oil shale with any chance of success."[17]

The problem of raising funds was complicated both by the stock promoter and by the lack of knowledge on the part of some of those involved. A 1920 article stated the problem this way:

"These few random instances indicate the ignorance that infests the 'literature' of American oil shale. Some men are both ignorant and crooked. Such men have exhibited pieces of apparatus said to be efficient retorts, but which could not, by any means, have been caused to educe oil from shale; they have claimed ownership of land that they had jumped simply for the purpose of a deal, with no possibility of securing title or possession; they have written glowing reports upon questionable processes and almost inaccessible tracts of oil-shale land. In short, they have wrought inestimable injury to the industry they have pretended to foster, and it is my hope that they will be eliminated in the revival that is surely coming. Ignoramuses and crooks have ever invaded enterprises, particularly in the beginning. But an industry such as the development and exploitation of oil shale cannot proceed or thrive except under the direction of honest and technically competent men."[18]

Several estimates were given as to the actual amount of capital needed to start an oil shale plant. In 1918, $2,500,000 was estimated; in 1919, the *Engineering and Mining Journal* gave figures of between $1,000,000 and $5,000,000; Gavin in 1920 estimated $1,000,000 would be needed for a Government-sponsored semi-commercial development program; Alderson's estimate of $500,000 was one of the lowest figures. Since plant capacity was not stated, the estimates are only of academic interest.

It is doubtful if any individual company spent as much as $500,000 on a plant in Colorado. The total spent by all Colorado companies probably did not exceed $1,000,000. Most of the companies ran out of money or their supporters were unwilling to invest more money in them, and mechanic liens were filed against the lands of the companies. By 1922, F. A. Wadleigh wrote that "the lack of money, plus inexperienced management, has been the chief cause of most of the failures."[19]

It is not surprising that these small companies were unable to raise sufficient capital. Established stock brokerage houses were not enthusiastic about selling stock for these oil shale companies. As one person stated:

"I am not going to be in a hurry about a Denver connection and do not think that many of the so-called standard houses will be interested at this stage of the industry. Denver brokers are great people to follow. . . ."[20]

Hardly any of the stock advertising pamphlets of oil shale companies bore a stockbroker's or underwriter's name or office. Most of them requested the reader to send the purchase money for the stock directly to the company's office or to obtain more information directly from the company. A few pamphlets named a fiscal agent. Some of these pamphlets indicated that the agent had the same address as the company.

The oil shale corporation usually issued all of their shares to one or more of the organizers in return for oil shale claims or the rights to a patent process or some other form of property. The organizers then would donate various amounts of such stock back to the corporation. This "treasury stock" would then be sold to the public.

Annual corporation reports of the following companies show that all, or substantially all, of their outstanding stock was issued for property: The Monarch Oil Shale Company, the American Shale Refining Company, the Colorado Carbon Company, The Columbia Oil Shale and Refining Company, The March Oil Shale Company, the Washington Shale Oil & Products Company, The Belvedere Oil Shale and Refining Company, The Overland Producing and Refining Company, and The Searchlight Oil Shale & Refining Company.

The treasury stock of the corporation, when sold, would be nonassessable even though sold below its par value. This practice of selling reacquired securities would protect the purchaser from any possible claims by creditors of the company (in the event the company failed) for the difference between the sale price and the par value of the stock. It also meant that the company would not have to disclose in its annual report how much stock was sold for cash. Many of these companies advertised their stock as treasury stock, fully paid and nonassessable. The officers of companies, seeking to raise more money through stock sales, did not have the criminal or civil sanctions of a Federal or State Securities Act to restrain their promotional representations.

GOLD, SILVER
AND OTHER METALS

A number of reports by private investigators claimed that gold, silver, platinum and zinc could be found in commercial quantities in oil shale. These claims were published in the literature, and two such claims are presented as examples of what the investors of the day would have had access to:

"*Placer Machine Recovers Free Gold from Oil Shale Deposits*

"Proof that gold in paying quantities exists in the oil shales of Colorado received further confirmation in a test made in Denver on August 17 [1922], in which a quantity of deoiled and decarbonized shale was subjected to treatment in a placer machine known as the Little Giant. This machine is the invention of Thomas F. Harkins, a pioneer mining man, and has been devised for the treatment of gravel deposits where the gold was too fine to be recovered by other methods. That the gold is in the shale and that it can be recovered by this equipment was plainly evident.

"The shale used in the test came from the properties of the Monarch Shale Oil Company, on Conn Creek, Garfield County, Colorado, and was first treated at the Ginet demonstration retort in Denver, under the supervision of J. H. Ginet, the inventor of the process. After treatment for oil, the spent shale was decarbonized in the same retort by the admission of air to the retort. It was then ground fine in a rod mill and run over the safety boxes of the placer machine. The recovery was in the form of hundreds of minute particles of flour gold. For the purpose of arriving at the actual quantity, the concentrates were submitted to W. E. Burlingame, prominent metallurgist and assayer of Denver, who furnished a report showing the recovery was at the rate of $2 per ton of raw shale. Pannings of the shale made later showed many colors that did not get into the concentrates. As the placer machine is a very simple device in which no quicksilver is used and the material is not subjected to chemicals, it is conceivable that the recovery represents only a fraction of the quantity that may be obtained by further treatment. The merit of the proposition from a commercial standpoint lies in the fact that the secondary operations after the oil is made are inexpensive. J. H. Ginet states that the crushing and decarbonizing as performed in his plant could be done for 30 cents a ton. The operation of the placer machine represents a very trifling expense, and it is believed that the total cost of treating spent shale for metal recovery cannot exceed 50 cents per ton. On a basis of only $2.00 per ton in value recovered, it will be seen that the margin of profit is wide, when consideration is taken of the fact that a barrel of oil has already been taken from the crude material.

"Interest in the present test attaches to the fact that it has been made by companies and individuals in no way connected with other concerns whose operations have been fully recounted in former issues of this magazine. In the last number there was printed a report on the runs of the American Continuous Retort in Denver, in which it was known that the shale treated carried values running from $3.24 to $5.59 in gold per ton of raw shale. The report was made by a reputable engineer and gave exact weights and final determinations. The decarbonized shale was treated with cyanide in apparatus not specially devised for the purpose. In test runs made a few months ago in retorts at Fort Wayne, Indiana, under the supervision of Dr. Frederick Salathe, noted refinery chemist, the engineer's report states that gold to the value of $7.50 per ton of raw shale was recovered. The shale treated came from Green River, Wyoming." [21]

The following was published in March 1920: [22]

"*Precious Metals, Gold, Silver and Platinum Recovered from Oil Shale*

    A. M. Beam, President
    F. D. Lewis, Sec. Treas.
    The American Continuous Retort
    Office, 807 Central Savings Bank Bld.,
    Laboratory 3338 W. 34th Ave., Denver,
    Colo. Sept. 2, 1919

"I hereby certify, that the samples assayed for R. E. McGee gave the following results per ton of 2,000 pounds. Gold at $20.00 oz.: Silver at $1.10 oz.: Platinum at $105.00 oz.: Zinc at 8¢ per lb.: Oil 15¢ per gal.: Ammonium Sulphate, 15¢ per lb.: Potash, 15¢ lb.

McGee Oil Shale

Gold	.15 oz.	$3.00	Potash	16 lbs.	$2.40
Silver	5.5 oz.	6.05	Ammonium Sul.	33 lbs.	4.95
Platinum	.05 oz.	5.25	Oil	41.5 gal.	6.22
Zinc	45 lbs.	3.60			

Total Value per ton $31.41

Assay No. 2   November 17, 1919

"I hereby do certify, that the samples assayed for Dr. H. D. Newton gave the following results per ton of 2000 pounds: Gold at $20.00 oz.: Silver at $1.28 oz.: Platinum at $135.00 oz.: Oil at 10¢ per gallon: Ammonium Sulfate, 10¢ per pound: Potash, 10¢ per lb.

Fire Process

Gold	.15 oz.	$3.00	Zinc	5 lbs.	$ .40
Silver	2.00 oz.	2.56	Ammonium Sul.	27 lbs.	2.70
Platinum	.03 oz.	4.05	Oil	33 gal.	3.30

Total Value per ton $17.71

Cyanide Process

Gold	.26 oz.	$5.20	Zinc	5 lbs.	$ .40
Silver	2.00 oz.	2.55	Ammonium Sul.	27 lbs.	2.70
Platinum	.03	4.05	Oil	33 gal.	3.30

Total Value per ton $19.90

A. M. Beam
Chemist in Charge

Reports such as these probably were responsible for the following being published in January 1922:[23]

"Reports have been made, by private investigators, that gold, silver, and platinum could be found in commercial quantities in oil shale. Much discussion ensued and conflicting reports were published. At the Colorado School of Mines, Dr. Albert H. Low, Professor of Chemistry, and John C. Williams, at the Experimental Plant, made a careful examination of oil shale for precious metals, but reached only negative conclusions. Finally the United States Bureau of Mines at the Salt Lake Station made a thorough investigation and reported in Serial 2413 by Superintendent Thomas Varley, that the precious metals—Gold, Silver, and Platinum did not occur in oil shale in commercial quantities."

Note that the claim for recovery of placer gold was published in September of 1922, some nine or ten months after the report by the Colorado School of Mines and the U.S. Bureau of Mines that oil shale did *not* contain commercial quantities of precious metals.

RETORTS AND RETORTING

The problem of developing and recovering oil from oil shale received early consideration, and the first retort in Colorado was constructed on Dry Fork, Northwest De Beque (Fig 5) by The Oil Shale Mining Company in 1917. The next few years saw hundreds of retorts invented and two or three dozen built, several of which produced oil.

Proven technology for retorting oil shale was limited to that used in Scotland where an industry had existed for many years, but where the shale was quite different from that in the western United States. Gavin noted that the trend in the development of oil shale retorts in this country is away from the Scottish type.[24]

Gavin listed the principal features of proposed American retorts by dividing them into several general types:

1. Horizontal retorts with conveyor systems for moving shale through the retorts and discharging it.
2. Inclined retorts with conveyors or agitators.
3. Continuous, externally-heated, vertical retorts.
4. Intermittent, externally-heated, vertical retorts.
5. Internally-heated retorts.
6. Horizontal or inclined, rotary cylindrical retorts.
7. Miscellaneous types of retorts.

A listing of oil shale processes proposed for use in the United States is shown in Table III.

When Hamor prepared Chapter 10 of *Oil Shale,*[26] published in October 1925, he did not include many of the retorts listed by Gavin. However, he did add the following: "G. A. Bronder retort, Brooklyn, N.Y.; Hartman Rotary Continuous Retort, Ashland, Ore.; National Rotary, J. B. Newberry, Buffalo, N.Y.; and the Trumble Oil Shale Cycle Distillation Plant, Alhambra, Calif."

Hamor and Gavin both noted that none of the processes listed have been operated on a scale sufficient to give much of an idea as to their feasibility under commercial conditions. Gavin added that many of them existed only on paper, or in the minds of their inventors, and that most of the types proposed had been tried and rejected by the Scottish operators as inefficient or impractical, or had been replaced by better methods. Although not condemning them because American and Scottish shales differ, he did suggest that those contemplating retorts would do well to find if what they proposed had been tried and, if tried and rejected, the reasons for doing so.

Although much of the literature related to the need for more reliance on Scottish operations, R. D. George[27] cited the following:

"Previous to the discovery of well oil in Pennsylvania, there were fifty or sixty plants in the United States and several in Canada distilling oil from black shales and low grade cannel and other coal. According to Redwood[28] these plants were

*Fig. 5—The first retort to produce shale oil in Colorado. Original Henderson plant of The Oil Shale Mining
Company near De Beque, Colorado. (From* The Shale Review, *Sept. 1920.)*

distributed as follows: One in Portland, one in New Bedford, four in Boston, one in Hartford, five in the environs of New York, eight or ten in western Pennsylvania, twenty-five in Ohio, eight in Virginia, six in Kentucky, and one in St. Louis. Shales at some of the plant localities carry only 4 to 10 percent of volatile matter or would yield 8 to 20 gallons per ton.''

Gavin, in Bulletin 210, stated that in 1860 there were 53 such companies as described above, and that many of the companies operated under license from The Young Company of Scotland.

In spite of the many reported processes and the many companies formed, only a very few actual retorts were erected in the oil shale fields. Some were erected in laboratories or plants in other locations, but

TABLE III

OIL SHALE PROCESSES PROPOSED FOR USE IN THE UNITED STATES

Name	Owner or Inventor	Address of Owner or Inventor
Anderson	Anderson Shale Oil Co.	160 S. Broadway, Denver, Colo.
Balcome	Balcome RiteWay Eng. Co.	St. Jons, New Brunswick
Bishop	Bishop, J. A.	1265 Lafayette St., Denver, Colo.
Boyle	Boyle, A. M.	Reno, Nev.
Brown	Brown, H. L.	Newark, N.J.
Bussey	Bussey, C. C.	Brooklyn, N.Y.
Catlin	Catlin, R. M.	Franklin Furnace, N.J.
Chew	Chew, L. F.	Denver, Colo.
Colorado Continuous	Krustinic, E. L.	Denver, Colo.
Crane	Crane, A. G.	Reno, Nev.
Day-Heller	The Day Co.	San Francisco, Calif.
DeBrey	Mock, S. A.	Salt Lake City, Utah
Del Monte	Prevost, C. A.	Washington, D.C.
Edwards-Parks	Edwards, T. H.	Denver, Colo.
Erickson	Rainbow Pet. Pro. Co.	Salt Lake City, Utah
Galloupe	Galloupe, J. H.	Denver, Colo.
Ginet	Ginet, J. H.	Denver, Colo.
Godfrey	Godfrey, H. H.	Los Angeles, Calif.
Hague	Hague, S. T.	Salt Lake City, Utah
Hoover-Brown	Amer. Coal By-Prod. Co.	Denver, Colo.
Jensen	Jensen, J. B.	Salt Lake City, Utah
Johns	Ind. Process Eng. Co.	St. Louis, Mo.
Lesley	Lesley, R. W.	Philadelphia, Penn.
McCaskell	McCaskell, J. A.	Salt Lake City, Utah
Noad	Noad, J.	Essex, England
Porter	Porter Process Co.	Denver, Colo.
Perry	Perry, W. P.	London, England
Prioleau	Prioleau	London, England
Randall	Randall, J. W. H.	New York, N.Y.
Robinson	Robinson, T.	Anaconda, Mont.
Rogers	Rogers, L. H.	New York, N.Y.
Ryan	Nat. Oil Mach. Co.	New York, N.Y.
Scott	Amer. Eng. Assoc.	Detroit, Mich.
Seaman Rotary	Seaman Wastewood Chem. Co.	New York, N.Y.
Simpson	Simpson, L.	Ottawa, Canada
Simplex	Mt. Logan Oil Shale Co.	De Beque, Colo.
Stalmann	Stalmann, O.	Salt Lake City, Utah
Shreves	Shreves, F. G.	Denver, Colo.
Stone	Stone, H. G.	Chicago, Ill.
Straight	Straight, H. R.	Adel, Iowa
Thurlow	Thurlow, E. W.	Victoria, Australia
Wallace	Wallace, G. W.	St. Louis, Mo.
Watson	Watson Shale Ref. Co.	Salt Lake City, Utah
Wingett	Troy-Amer. Ret. Co.	Denver, Colo.
Whittaker-Prichard	Fuel Products Co.	New York, N.Y.
Young	Young, A. V.	De Beque, Colo.

This list was only of retorts or processes known to Gavin in July 1921 when he prepared this part of his report.[25]

available records indicate these produced very little shale oil. The actual retorts erected on field sites during the 1917–1930 period appear to have been as follows: one in Canada; one in Montana; two in Nevada; four in Utah; and seven in Colorado, one of which was a U.S. Government operation.

A number of these oil shale operations were legitimate. The companies were sincerely interested in developing an oil shale industry. Unfortunately, most found that getting oil from oil shale in quantity and at reasonable cost was much more difficult than they had anticipated. Their problems were compounded by the fact that most of the companies were small, often 4–8 men with additional labor hired when funds were available. Capital usually was limited, technical competence generally was lacking and roads were few and of poor quality, making access to the shale areas difficult. Most supplies had to be shipped in by rail before being hauled by truck, or team and wagon, to the construction site. On-site operations often were in isolated and remote areas that required living quarters for personnel, further compounding the financial and supply problems. The oil shale ore usually was in outcrops on near-vertical canyon walls at elevations from one to several thousand feet above the retort site (Fig 6). In one case, the miners lived in a section of the mine

Fig. 6—On the La Paz group near Grand Valley, Colorado. (From U.S. Geological Survey.)

rather than make the long trip from the retort and campsite to the mine each day. A few mines had cable tramways or inclined-rail tramways. These were used to transport oil shale to the retort and supplies to the mine. Safety rules prohibited men from riding; but these often were broken. Enforcement may have become easier after an inclined surface-rail car ran wild and several men were killed.

Although all of the listed factors contributed to the failure to establish even a small oil shale industry, the two key items appear to have been lack of capital and lack of technical knowledge by those involved. Marketing of the product, although a factor, was considered of minor importance because marketable quantities of shale oil were produced only by the Catlin Operation in Nevada where funds and technology were better than in other operations. It should be noted that *no major company* or organization of any sort became involved in the early development and production of western shale oil in the period 1917 to 1930, with the exception of the U.S. Government at its Rulison operation.

The problems of shale oil production might eventually have been solved if the need for the product had increased. However, new discoveries of oil in California, Texas and Oklahoma were made, and by 1924 the price of crude oil had dropped to less than half its 1920 level. Interest in oil shale decreased and by 1930, when the immense East Texas oil field was developed, not a single oil shale plant remained in operation.

PART II

1915–1930

The Boom Era

SHALE OIL PRODUCTION 1915-1930

While the lack of financial backing was an important factor, the absence of actual results in the form of oil production was also an important element in the failure of these early plants. According to reports filed with the Colorado Bureau of Mines and according to the Department of the Interior's "Mineral Resources" no appreciable amount of shale oil was produced or shipped from 1915 to 1921. From other evidence available, the Continental Oil Shale and Refining Company may have produced a little shale oil during its test runs in 1920; the Mount Logan Oil Shale Mining and Refining Company made some test runs in 1920; and The Oil Shale Mining Company shipped a few barrels of oil in 1920.

The year 1921 was the most productive of these early years. About 223 barrels of shale oil were produced: The Oil Shale Mining Company produced 30 barrels;[29] The Monarch Oil Shale Company, 71 barrels;[30] The Mount Logan Oil Shale and Refining Company, 52 barrels.[31]

The Colorado Carbon Company's reported production of 70 barrels[32] occurred either in Denver or Kansas City, because there never was a retort on the field property.

In 1922, the Index Oil Shale Company produced a small amount of oil. The Washington Shale Oil & Products Company and The Wyoming Oil Products Company reached the production stage in the late 1920s. No records could be found of production by the Utah retorts, although it is believed that token amounts of oil were produced by both the Willow Creek retort and by The Western Shale Oil Company. The retort of The Ute Oil Company apparently never operated. The Nevada operation of Catlin produced over 12,000 barrels of shale oil and refined products. The Montana and New Brunswick, Canada, operations produced a few barrels of oil each.

The literature indicates confusion among oil shale enthusiasts as to what the end-product from oil shale would be.

Crude shale oil, itself, was not marketable.

C. L. Jones of the Mellon Foundation argued for a staple product, presumably gasoline, kerosene or lubricating oil.[33] Some companies, such as The Oil Shale Mining Company, actually produced soap and sheep dip and advertised that wood preservers, roofing material, ointment and dandruff treatment could be made out of oil shale.[34] The Colorado Carbon Company's president spoke of varnishes, roof materials, 14 different acids, 12 different drugs, 24 dyes, 8 explosives, lard and soft rubber that would be made from shale oil.[35] Problems of use for oil shale never developed because of limited production. By 1930 no attempts were being made to produce shale oil, and this phase of the development was history.

Retorts were constructed and operated by a few companies. Other companies were only interested in obtaining oil shale land. Some obtained shale claims but for a variety of reasons never reached the point of conducting field experiments.

For the purpose of illustrating the events that took place, those companies and organizations mentioned most often in the literature are described in more detail in the following chapters.

Figure 7 shows location of Colorado oil shale area with respect to Denver.

Figure 8 is a map of Rifle, Grand Valley and De Beque area of Colorado showing approximate locations of the 1915-1930 oil shale operations described on the following pages.

COLORADO ACTIVITIES

American Continuous Retort Co.

This Denver, Colorado company claimed to recover

precious metals and was considered a questionable enterprise by many.

Organized	:	Unknown
Capitalized	:	$25,000–250,000 shares at 10 cents. Offer treasury stock at $5.00 per share
President	:	A. M. Beam
Vice-President	:	Walter McBride
Secretary-Treasurer	:	F. D. Lewis
Location	:	Denver, Colorado
Property	:	Unknown
Plant	:	Small plant in Denver
Mine	:	None
Production	:	None

The *National Petroleum News* of September 1920 describes this operation as follows:

"The American Continuous Retort Company, Denver, Colorado, F. D. Lewis, Secretary-Treasurer, patentee and general superintendent. Extensive ore treating plant nearing completion, equipped with latest designed appliances for treatment to point of greatest extraction of all ores, including shales and coals for recovery of hydrocarbons and by-products. A solid steel and brick retort for oil shale should be ready for operation by October 1, with cyanide and acid tanks for recovery of any mineral content after the oil ammonia and potash extraction has occurred. The retort consists of many horizontal steel shelves or plates through which the crushed shale is forced and agitated by baffle-plates, with numerous gas vents; the released gases going into water condensers. This retort and accessories, after the demonstration run, will be shipped to

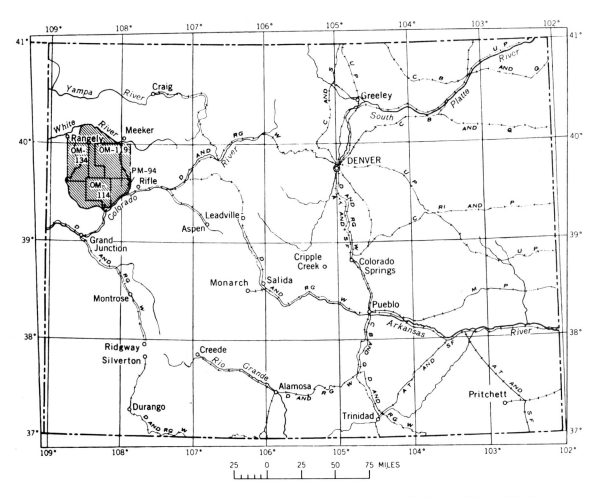

Fig. 7—Areal location of Piceance Creek Basin with respect to Denver, Colorado. (From U.S. Geological Survey Bulletin 1082L.)

Western Colorado for commercial operation by a Denver shale corporation. Two car-loads of massive shale from the De Beque district, sent by J. W. Hess, of Pueblo, will be used in the first run made by this plant. Shales from Kentucky, Texas and other states will also be treated. This combination plant is the largest and of the heaviest construction in every respect of any in this country, the electric wiring alone costing $12,000 and is continuous throughout, the plant covering a block in length. Mr. Lewis is disposing of no stock, is amply financed, has been in many mineral areas of both continents, holds patents to all his processes and is exclusively engaged in treating ores for the trade and the construction and installation of plants for all ores demonstrated susceptible of profitable extraction. Mr. Lewis says he has found various precious minerals in profitable quantities in oil shales.''

Mr. Charles L. Jones in the *Mellon Institute Report,* October 13, 1920, reported as follows:

"This company claims to secure precious metal values varying from $20.00 upward per ton of shale. They distill off the oil, then oxidize the carbon out of the residue, then amalgamate and cyanide. The company has been fairly successful in enlisting support, as strangers are invited to come into their laboratory and make assays under their direction (and using their cyanide and mercury) to prove the presence of the values they claim.''

Mr. Jones also intimated that the Colorado Shales and Metals Company, Denver, and the Wyoming Shales and Metals Company of Salt Lake City, Utah, were part of, or associated with, the American Continuous Retort Company.

The Company Assay Office provided the following statement to the American Continuous Retort Company, and it was released by the company to the public:[36]

"I hereby certify that the sample for the shale oil company gave the following results per ton of 2000 pounds. Gold at $20 per ounce, Silver at $1.00 per ounce, Platinum at $108 per ounce, Oil, 20¢ per gal., Ammonium Sulphate at 20¢ per lb., Zinc at 7¢ per pound, Potash, 29¢ per pound.

1. Continental Shale Oil & Refining Company
2. Columbia Oil Shale & Refining Company
3. Union Oil Company of California
4. Bureau of Mines (Anvil Points)
5. Bureau of Mines (Rulison Operation)
6. Champion Shale Company
7. March Oil Shale Company
8. Grand Valley Oil & Shale Company
9. Mt. Logan Oil Shale & Refining Company
10. Monarch Oil Shale Company
11. Lackawanna Shale Products Company
12. Washington Shale and Products Company
13. American Shale Refining Company
14. Campbell Refining Company
15. Searchlight Oil Shale & Refining Company
16. Index Shale Company
17. (The) Oil Shale Mining Company
18. Belvedere Oil Shale & Refining Company
19. Colorado Carbon Company

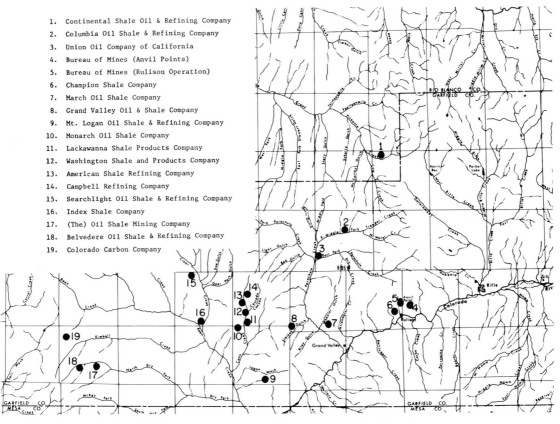

Fig. 8—Location of Colorado oil shale activities 1915–1930. (By author.)

"Big flat piece, shale; Gold .22 oz., Silver $4.50, Platinum .04 oz., Oil 70.5 gal., Ammonium Sulphate 17.4 lbs., Zinc, x; Potash, 50¢. Total value $36.63."

And:

"Denver, Colo., Dec. 5, 1917—We hand you here with the results we found after carefully checking your samples of oil shale:

"Gold— .38 oz., Silver @ $5.00	= $12.10
Platinum— .08 oz., $108 per oz.	= $ 8.64
Potash 1.03%, 26 lbs., @ 20¢ per lb.	= $ 5.20
Oil 71.43 gallons at 20¢	= $14.86
Ammonium Sulfate—20 lbs. @ 20¢	= $ 4.00
Total Value	= $44.80"

There is no evidence that the retort described (Fig 9) was ever moved from Denver or that it ever operated to any extent.

This company was not mentioned in the literature surveyed after 1921.

American Shale Refining Company

This company was also known as the Troy-American Petroleum Company.

Organized	:	1917 or 1918 (An Arizona Corporation)
Capitalized	:	$500,000 (50,000 shares at $10.00 each)
President	:	J. L. Warren
Vice-President	:	L. L. Aiken
Secretary-Treasurer	:	C. C. Dillard
Location	:	Conn Creek
Property	:	4480 acres
Plant	:	Proposed use of a Wingett retort. Retort was constructed but never erected on site.
Mine	:	None
Production	:	None

This company was located on Conn Creek in the De Beque district and owned 4480 acres. *The Colorado School of Mines Quarterly* for 1919 reported:

Fig. 9—Rod mill of the American continuous retort, Denver, Colorado. (From The Shale Review, *April,* 1922.)

Fig. 10—A tramway tower of the American Shale Refining Company, Conn Creek, Colorado. (1978 photograph by author.)

"The company is erecting a 150-ton [per day] retort. The cost of this retort was $40,000; succeeding retorts will probably cost $15,000 each. They will be placed 200 feet above the creek level to give ample dumping ground. The process of distillation and refining has been worked out by the company's chemist and has engaged his time for the past two years. The material for a 3,000 foot tram is now on the ground. The capacity of the tram is 900 tons a day—sufficient to supply shale to six 150-ton retorts. The shale cliffs at the camp rise to a height of 2500 feet. In these cliffs are the outcropping of five well defined oil strata, but only the two richest will be worked at present. From the camp, the outcroppings of the rich shale can be seen at seven different exposures. The first and richest is 200 feet below the summit of the cliff. This seam is sixty feet thick and is expected from extensive tests made by the company, that the beds are horizontal, lying in a great knob, or outlier, so that their extent can easily be determined. The first stratum, as a whole, is estimated by the company to contain 9,000,000 barrels of crude oil and 9,000 tons of ammonium sulphate;

the second 10,000,000 barrels of crude oil and 10,000 tons of ammonium sulphate. The company has expended to March 1, 1918, $83,101.00 in the development and equipment of its property."

Mr. C. L. Jones described this operation in his October 1920 report to the Mellon Institute as follows:

"The attempt of the American Shale Refining Co., Denver, to develop a shale retorting process is worthy of mention. This Company, composed of officers of the Midwest Oil Co., employed Mr. Wingett of the latter company to design for them an oil shale retort during 1918. The retort was designed, built, and set up in a Denver foundry. It was then shipped to the property of the company on Conn Creek, near De Beque, when the death of the president S. P. Barron, halted the work. The castings have been lying on the ground since the summer of 1918, and no effort has been made to complete the plant, although before work was discontinued a retort site had been excavated, and an aerial tramway well begun.

"As nearly as can be judged from the castings which litter the ground, the retort is a vertical cylinder some 8 feet in diameter by 20 feet high, made up of shallow compartments 2 feet deep. Alternate compartments seem to be occupied by combustion space and retorting space. A series of rakes fastened to a central shaft stir the shale. In design the retort is somewhat like the Wedge mechanical roaster, used for roasting ores."

The tramway referred to by Jones was obtained from Aspen, Colorado, where it had been abandoned for some time when it was purchased in 1917. Four towers were erected and cable was installed in part. The tramway was never operated.[37] Figure 10 shows the remains of a tramway tower on the property. *The Shale Review* of 1919[38] reported that the Company had a good camp, but that the retort had not been erected.

On the death of S. P. Barron in 1920, control of the company passed to the Troy-American Petroleum Corporation, which also controlled the Troy Oil & Gas and the Xetloc Oil Companies, operating in various fields in Wyoming and Oklahoma.[39]

No further mention of activities by Troy-American Petroleum Corporation or by American Shale Refining Company was noted in the literature.

The Belvedere Oil Shale and Refining Company

Most of the organizers and officers of this company were from Montana and Minnesota and the company was authorized to sell stock in Montana.

Organized	:	October 14, 1919 in the State of Colorado
Capitalized	:	$300,000 to $1,000,000 with a $1.00 per share value
President	:	W. L. Turner
Vice-President	:	S. R. Hartley
Treasurer	:	A. V. Young
Location	:	On upper Dry Fork about 25 miles from De Beque
Property	:	640 to 1560 acres
Plant	:	Young retort on property (1923)
Mine	:	No record of mine
Production	:	None recorded

Belvedere was a Colorado Corporation with a license to sell stock in Montana.[40] An attempt to obtain permission to sell its stock in Minnesota was rejected by the Public Securities Commission of Minnesota in February 1920 because the Commission felt:

"... that the oils shale business in this country is in the purely experimental stage and no company so far has demonstrated that the product of oil from shale be made a commercial success. Under the circumstances we believe that a license to sell stock cannot be granted to your company."[41]

A. V. Young, Treasurer of Belvedere, was the inventor of the Young retort. Young also was a superintendent for The Oil Shale Corporation (in no way related to The Oil Shale Corporation organized in 1956 and now the TOSCO Corporation) also located on Dry Fork and for whom he was working when he developed his retort. The Young retort was abandoned by The Oil Shale Corporation in 1919. However, a Young retort was reported to be on the Belvedere property in 1923. There is no record that the retort was ever installed and operated. A tramway was reported completed, except for installation of the buckets, by late 1919 when winter closed the operation. There is no record that the tramway was ever completed. It is doubtful if the company ever had sufficient operating funds.[42] The company became defunct October 23, 1925.

Bureau of Mines—Rulison Project

In 1913, the U.S. Bureau of Mines began to investigate the oil shale deposits in Colorado, Utah, Wyoming, Montana and California, primarily to establish the basis for segregation of land, and secondarily to ascertain the extent, character and commercial value of the land deposits. Martin J. Gavin[43] described the early work of the Bureau as follows:

"... Work ... during 1918 consisted largely in the collection and compilation of all available information on the subject of oil shale ... Early in 1919 research work was begun at the Salt Lake City Experimental Station of the Bureau of Mines and has been continuing there. In November 1919 an oil shale section of the Bureau was officially established at the Salt Lake Station. In February 1920, under a co-operative agreement entered into by the Bureau of Mines and the State of Colorado, investigational work was begun at the state oil inspection laboratories, University of Colorado, Boulder. The governor of Colorado allotted a fund of $10,000.00 for this co-operative work ... In May of this year (1920) the state of Utah authorized the expenditure of a similar fund for oil shale investigations ... the Bureau of Mines has been investigating oil shales as well as its limited funds would permit, and has requested Congress for an appropriation of $170,000 for the

Fig. 11—View of Rulison oil shale mine as it appeared in 1976. (Courtesy of Roger J. Runk, Anvil Points, Colorado.)

erection, equipping and operation of an oil shale experimental station . . .''

In 1925, an appropriation of $90,000 was made by Congress to the Bureau of Mines for the ''. . . development of oil shale, including the construction of necessary plant, purchase or mining of shale, operation of plant, etc. This appropriation was made largely on the recommendation of the President's Naval Oil Committee to determine the possibility of securing a future source of fuel for the Navy.''[44]

''The appropriation became available March 4, 1925. The site selected was in Secs. 22 and 26, T6S., R95W. The plant site was on Naval Oil Shale Reserve No. 3, and the mine on Naval Oil Shale Reserve No. 1. (The plant site was about 11 miles west of Rifle, Colorado, and about 1.5 miles north of the highway). The mine was about 2100 ft. in elevation above the plant site and 5600 ft. slope distance from it. The site was officially approved on October 3, 1925, when plant construction began.''

The original plans contemplated erection of one or two retorts of commercial size at a representative site. The program involved mining, producing oil under various retorting conditions and studying the oils produced. Refining studies were to be made of the oils produced in cooperation with research institutes and petroleum refining companies.

The plant consisted of two retorts, machine shop, storehouse and boilerhouse combined, combination office, laboratory and bunk house, control house and mess house. The main camp buildings were wooden-frame structures with celotex siding and lining and tar-paper roofs. The mess house and plant buildings were steam heated and electric power for lights and other uses was provided. The mine was intended to supply shale without attempting to experiment with mining methods. Most of the shale was obtained by bench quarrying, although a short adit (Fig 11) was run in the zone of richer shales. The rich shales and leaner quarry shales were mixed before use (Fig 12).

Before a decision was made to erect a tramway to convey shale from the mine to the plant, formal bids were obtained from local packing contractors on hauling the shale by pack train. The proposals submitted to the packers requested bids on:

''Transporting, by pack train, a distance of approximately 3 miles, down hill over 15 to 20 percent grade, from mine site on Naval Oil Shale Reserve No. 1, to plant site on Naval Oil Shale Reserve No. 3, near Rulison, Colo., 4,000 tons of oil shale at a minimum rate of 7½ tons per day, over a period of 15 months commencing April 1, 1926; shale to be delivered in sewed bags to pack train at mine and accepted in sewed bags at plant site, sacks to average 100 to 110 pounds each.

Fig. 12—Rulison oil shale mine ore bins and tramway loading area as they appeared in 1976. (Courtesy *Roger J. Runk, Anvil Points, Colorado.*)

"Alternate bid: Transporting same quantity under same conditions except that shale will be delivered in loose form to pack train and accepted in loose form at plant site, shale to be broken to approximately 6 inches in diameter."[45]

"The lowest bid for sewed bags was $15,000 ($3.50 per ton). Only one packer considered packing the loose shale, and his bid was $18,000 ($4.50 per ton). Tramway cost was estimated not to exceed $18,000 (actual cost $17,923, including storage bins at mine and plant). Other considerations such as getting supplies to the mine, the need for a crusher at the mine, bad weather and slipperiness of the trail, led to a decision in favor of the tram. Tramway machinery was ordered October 9, 1925 and construction was completed and tram [put] in operation September 11, 1926. While some problems developed [its] operation was considered as satisfactory."[46]

The mine plant consisted of a shop, bunk house and mess house. These buildings were of the wooden frame celotex-side type, except the mine mess house which was of galvanized iron. The roofs of all mine buildings were galvanized iron over two-inch boards. Ore-bin and loading facilities for the tramway were built of heavy timber construction.

As previously stated, the major portion of the shale used was obtained by open quarry mining of the outcrop. No mining difficulties were encountered in either the quarry or small underground adit, except those caused by bad weather.

The retorts selected were thought to be the most suitable for the experimental work planned. The two retorting units (Fig 13) were: (1) A single-unit Pumpherston retort, rated capacity 5 tons per day and (2) an N-T-U (Nevada, Texas, Utah) retort, rated capacity 20 tons per charge.

The Pumpherston retort had been used in commercial shale oil production in Scotland for nearly 30 years, and also was used successfully in France, Spain and Australia. A standard Pumpherston retort was composed of two main sections one above the other, the upper one being constructed of iron 15 feet high, the lower one of fire brick 20 feet high. Shale is fed in at the top and there in the iron section is subjected to heat from 750°F to 900°F, distilling the oil and gas. The shale then is let down to the lower, or fire-brick, section where it is subjected to a temperature of 1300°F, or more. Steam is injected and ammonia is produced when hydrogen in the steam unites with nitrogen in the shale. (Complete details of operational procedures and equipment may be found in Bulletin 315.[43])

Heat-curing of the retort began on October 23, 1926, and the first shale was charged to the retort on

September 17; the first oil was produced a few hours later during the night. Operation of the retort continued except for periods when all work was recessed. In general, results were satisfactory, the retort handled without difficulty all shales that did not exhibit strong coking tendencies in the assay report.

The N-T-U retort, the second type selected for experimentation, was a direct-heating process, rather than the indirect heating process of the Pumpherston and of all other field retorts of the 1917–1930 era with the exception of one of the Catlin, Nevada, retorts. In the direct-heating process, the combustion of the gas and the carbon of the spent shale takes place within the retort itself, steam or gases heated outside the retort proper may be passed through the retort in direct contact with the shale charge.

Material and equipment for the N-T-U retort were ordered from the N-T-U Co. (Gotham National Bank Building, New York, N.Y.) on May 26, 1926, and were delivered to Rulison during the last week in June. The

Fig. 13—View of completed Pumpherston retort and construction of N-T-U retort (tank-like object center left) at Bureau of Mines Rulison Project. (Boyd Guthrie photograph—1925. U.S. Bureau of Mines.)

Fig. 14—Some of the early oil shalers employed at the Bureau of Mines Rulison Project. Boyd Guthrie is on the left of the first row. (Boyd Guthrie photograph—1928. U.S. Bureau of Mines.)

retort was completed on October 14, 1926, except for the gas exhauster which was installed early in November. The first test run was started on January 17, 1927. (Details of construction and operation are presented in Bulletin 315.[43])

From January 17 through June 26, 1927, 29 runs were made and a total of 788 tons of shale were put through the retort. The total oil recovered was 13,750 gallons, an average of 17.5 gallons per ton of shale retorted. Operation of this retort continued during the life of the Rulison project, and its performance was considered satisfactory. Figure 14 shows some of the plant crew. Boyd Guthrie was later to direct the Bureau's Rifle Project.

Refinery tests showed that the oils produced by the two methods of retorting were essentially similar, except that oil from the internally fired retort (N-T-U) contained a smaller amount of secondary decomposition products than that produced by the externally fired Pumpherston retort. The sulfur content of both the crude and distilled fractions was high. Refinery losses for all products were higher, and cracking yields lower, than from petroleum distillates or residuums. The results of the refinery studies did not favor shale oil as a substitute for petroleum.

Modifications were made to the plant in 1928 on the basis of earlier operations, and the results of the subsequent 1928-29 operations were much more satisfactory.

Oil shale treated and shale oil produced during operations of the Rulison plant were as follows:

Retort	Year	Shale Processed (tons)	Oil Produced (gallons)
N-T-U	1926	200	3,360
N-T-U	1927	800	13,774
N-T-U	1928	936	22,207
N-T-U	1929	1,447	46,197
	Total N-T-U	3,383 tons	85,538 gallons
Pumpherston	Sept. 1926–June 30, 1927	1,100	20,000
Pumpherston	1928	1,189	29,739
Pumpherston	1929–closed April 29	501	14,593
	Total Pumpherston	2,790 tons	64,332 gallons

During the 1926–29 operation of the Rulison Project, 6,173 tons of oil shale were processed to produce 149,870 gallons, or 3,568 barrels of shale oil. The project was closed June 30, 1929, and all equipment removed. Figure 15 shows the plant site as it appeared in 1977.

Campbell Refining Corp.

This company is included as an example of what may have been one of the more obvious stock promotions of the day.

Organized   :   April 5, 1919, a
                     Delaware Corporation

Fig. 15—U.S. Bureau of Mines' plant site as it appeared in 1976. (Courtesy of Roger J. Runk, Anvil Points, Colorado.)

Capitalized	:	$3,000,000 at $10 per share
President	:	C. Albert Campbell —also General Mgr.
Vice-President	:	Richard P. Stakelum
Secretary-Treasurer	:	Cyrus J. Rankin
Property	:	1760 acres
Location	:	Conn Creek
Plant	:	None—advertised "Rankin" retort and production
Mine	:	None
Production	:	None

The Campbell Refining Corporation appears to have been entirely a stock promotion. The company, in its 1922 report to the Colorado Bureau of Mines, reported owning 1760 acres of land, doing assessment work and constructing trails and cabins.

A copy of a letter from the Mayor of the Town of De Beque to Mr. O. J. Berry of Glenwood Springs[47] is reproduced on a subsequent page to show that officers of the Campbell Refining Corporation had limited knowledge of this oil shale area and that their reputation had preceded them (Fig 16).

In July 1921, J. S. Scott of Paterson, New Jersey, wrote to Professor Hunter, State Oil Inspectors

TOWN OF DE BEQUE

DE BEQUE, COLORADO

OFFICE OF THE TOWN CLERK   May 16,1922.

Mr, O.J.Berry.

    Glenwood Spgs., Colo.,

Dear Mr. Berry:

       Mr. Cyrus J. Rankin turned up here yesterday and hired Berry Cameron to show him some shale lands at 4 P.M. He interviewed the local newspaper man later and gave him some dope to run.

       To my knowledge this is the first time he has ever been in De Beque but Mr. Campbell has been here several times. They have no lands here that I know of.

       Their letter head reads-- Campbell Refining Corp.--Camreco Brand Petroleum Products.--250 West 57th St. N.Y.--C.Albert Campbell Pres.- Cyrus J.Rankin Treas.   They claim holdings called THE BLUE BIRD Triumph,PART CLEAR CREEK --and BIG BELL--Some 1760 acres. I think this lies above Ginet's Monarch Co. Land on Conn Creek.

       He left presumably for Glenwood last night after talking about some litigation with Hubbard,stating he would be back here on Thursday again and having some write ups in recent Gd. Jct.Papers.

       This Campbell Co. is the one I spoke to you about a couple of years ago that sold stock in K.C., Okla.,and Chicago and Buffalo claiming they had a 1000 ton retort in operation here producing 200 bbls a day.

       Yesterday was the first time I have ever laid eyes on Rankin here and is his first and only appearance as far as I know,but it is not to be found that he saw any shale managers yesterday.

    I will be pleased to meet the gentleman if he comes Thursday.

       Yours Truly,

       Lewis W Leach.
       Mayor.

He has his own process and claims to have built one in N.Y. also.

Fig. 16—Town of DeBeque, Colorado, letter regarding Campbell Refining Corporation. (From U.S. Department of Interior.)

CAMPBELL REFINING CORPORATION
CONVERTIBLE 8% GOLD COUPON BONDS

Authorized Issue $500,000.oo

Dated July 1st, 1920   Maturing July 1st, 1935

Interest payable semi-annually, July 1st and January 1st. Principal, interest and participation in earnings payable in New York. Coupon Bonds in denominations of $1,000, $500 and $100, with privilege of registration as to principal. Redeemable as a whole or in part on any interest date on 60 days' notice at one hundred and ten (110) and accrued interest.

CAMPBELL REFINING CORPORATION was organized under the laws of the State of Delaware for the purpose of engaging in the business of refining petroleum, and in the transportation and marketing of petroleum products.

Authorized Capital 300,000 Shares

150,000 Shares Preferred	150,000 Shares Common
PAR Value $10.00	PAR Value $10.00
Issued and outstanding	42,000 Shares Preferred
	42,000 " Common
Unissued and Treasury Stock	108,000 Shares Preferred
	108,000 " Common

The corporate proceedings in connection with the issue of these Bonds were under the supervision of and have been approved by Dudley A. Wilson, Attorney, 111 Broadway, New York City.

Price, $100.00 and accrued interest

CAPITAL ISSUES FUNDING CO., Inc.
50 EAST 42nd STREET
NEW YORK CITY

Fig. 17—(a) (b) and (c): Prospectus, Campbell Refining Corp. (From U.S. Department of Interior.)

CAMPBELL REFINING CORPORATION
(Incorporated under the laws of the State of Delaware)

MANAGEMENT
The management of the Corporation is under the close supervision of experienced oil men:

C. ALBERT CAMPBELL, President and General Manager, has been identified with the oil industry for more than 20 years.

CYRUS J. RANKIN, Secretary and Treasurer, an expert mechanical engineer, is in charge of plant construction.

RICHARD P. STAKELUM, Vice-President, an oil man who is thoroughly familiar with the marketing of petroleum products.

PURPOSE OF ISSUE
These Bonds were issued to provide funds for the installation of production and refining equipment and marketing of gasoline, motor oils, lubricants, waxes, greases, etc., from the crude material of which the Corporation owns a positive supply to insure a daily production of three thousand barrels for twenty years. Oils and gasoline thus far produced are of the very highest quality.

SECURITY
The Bonds constitute a direct obligation of the Corporation, and are secured by properties owned by the Corporation conservatively estimated at $3,000,000, and upon the completion of the plants and refinery, pipe lines, etc., the properties securing this issue of Bonds will be well worth $5,000,000. Title to these properties is recorded in Book No. 124, page 95 thereof, in the County Clerk's Office, at Glenwood Springs, County Seat of Garfield County, Colorado. The properties are unencumbered excepting this Bond issue.

EARNINGS
It is conservatively estimated that on a basis of the initial capacity net earnings, after making allowance for depreciation, etc., will amount to about $2,500,000, equal to over seven times interest charges on the entire capitalization and Bonded indebtedness of the Corporation.

PARTICIPATION IN EARNINGS
20% of the Net Earnings of the preceding calendar year after deducting taxes, interest charges, sinking fund requirements and cumulative Preferred and Common Stock dividends is to be distributed among the Bond holders until such time as the Bonds are redeemed, or converted into Preferred and Common Stock of the Company, as set forth in said Bonds.

CONVERSION OF BONDS
Bonds may be converted at the option of the holders, on or before July 1st, 1923, on the basis of $100 par value of Preferred Capital Stock, and $50 par value of Common Capital Stock for each $100 par value in Bonds so converted.

PREFERRED STOCK PROVISIONS
The Preferred Shares confer the right to a fixed Cumulative dividend at the rate of 10% per annum, and rank as regards return of capital in priority of Common Shares. On any dividend date after 30 days advertised notice, the Corporation at its option may redeem the whole or a part of the Preferred Stock by the payment of $11.50 per share and accrued dividends.

BUSINESS PROSPECTS
With conservative capitalization, well-equipped properties, the best of managerial supervision, unlimited supply of raw material, broad and well developed markets and demand in excess of production, the prospects of CAMPBELL REFINING CORPORATION for the coming years indicate unusual opportunities for success.

Fig. 17—(b) continued.

ESTIMATED COST OF CONSTRUCTION AND OPERATION

Production Equipment $212,000.00
Power Plant 17,000.00
Recovery and Condensing Plant 31,000.00
Miscellaneous Equipment 2,000.00
Contingencies and Engineering—20% 52,400.00

COST $314,400.00
Cost of refinery including filtering and barreling houses, stills, condensers, agitators, tankage, bleachers, filters, etc. 280,000.00

ESTIMATED TOTAL COST PRODUCTION AND REFINERY EQUIPMENT $594,400.00

REVENUE

Basis for annual revenue production of 350,000 bbls. Crude Oil
—1 bbl. 42-Gal. and refining records:

GASOLINE	15%—460 End Point	6.30 @ 20c	$1.26
KEROSENE	5%—40.0 Be. Gravity	2.10 @ 14c	.29
GAS OIL	18%	7.56 @ 10c	.75
SPINDLE OIL	9%—33.5 Be. Gravity	3.78 @ 30c	1.13
	355 Flash—400 Fire		
	Viscosity 158 @ 70″ F		
MOTOR OIL	36%—30.0 Be. Gravity	15.12 @ 40c	6.00
	400 Flash—460 Fire		
	Viscosity 228 @ 70″ F		
SLACK WAX	2%	Lb 8.4 @ 12c	1.00
PITCH	5%	2.10 @ 10c	.21

Value per ton—42 Gals. $10.64
Total value yearly production 350,000 bbls. x $10.64 .... $3,724,000.00

EXPENSES

Fixed Charges

Interest on $594,400.00 @ 8% $47,552.00
Taxes Estimated 7,500.00
Production Plant Operating Expenses 555,000.00
Maintenance, renewals and repairs to plant, 10% 31,440.00
REFINERY OPERATING EXPENSES 265,460.00
Maintenance, renewals and repairs, 10% 28,000.00
GENERAL OVERHEAD EXPENSES 121,000.00

TOTAL FIXED CHARGES AND COST OPERATION OF PRODUCTION AND REFINERY PLANTS $1,055,952.00

NET RECEIPTS OVER AND ABOVE 8% INTEREST ON INVESTMENT EXCLUSIVE OF MARKETING COSTS $2,668,048.00

The information and statistics given in this circular are not guaranteed, but they constitute the data upon which we have based this issue, and have been secured from official sources which we believe to be accurate and reliable.

Fig. 17—(c) continued.

Office, Denver, Colorado. His letter follows in part:

"...The Statements, as published are disappoint-in view of the state[ment] made in this part of the country, by the representative of the 'Campbell Refining Corporation' who states that the company have 1760 acres of oil shale land at De Beque, Garfield County, Colorado. That they have a 10 inch pipe line from the reduction works to the mill a distance of 17 miles and that they are operating their plant on a commercial basis and are producing 100 bbls. of crude oil a day on a production of 60 gallons from each ton of shale. They state also that recently a new use has been found for the waste, or residue, which makes it worth $14.00 a ton.

"The reports above referred to were dated June, July, Aug. and Oct. of last year (1921) . . ."[48]

In July 1921, the State Inspectors of Oils sent a copy of Mr. Scott's letter to Mr. McEniry, U.S. Land Office, Denver, that stated:

"I have already communicated with Mr. Lindland [of] the Post Office Inspectors, and are hoping that he will take some action that will make those responsible for such wicked swindles, at last suffer for them."[49]

Stock sales in New York and the East were reported to have exceeded one million dollars.

A part of the company literature (Fig 17) is reproduced as an illustration of what the public presentation claimed. The information shown is fairly typical of the day, and in itself was difficult to evaluate as to validity or intent. This operation, along with many others, was not mentioned in the literature reviewed after 1922.

Colorado School of Mines

Dr. Victor C. Alderson, President of the Colorado School of Mines during the early period of oil shale interest, was highly active in the effort to develop oil shale. Dr. Alderson wrote many articles for publication in the literature of the time, including at least one book on the subject.[50] In view of its President's interest, it was logical that the School also would become involved, and it did. The following article summarized such interests:

"At the Colorado School of Mines, oil shale experimental work has been in progress since 1917. The school quarterlies have frequently treated of the subject. An oil shale laboratory has been equipped not only for experimental work but also for instruction purposes. The school has organized a four-year petroleum degree—the only one

in the United States—within which is included courses in the techniques of oil shale. The school thus recognizes not only the technical and economic features of the subject but also the necessity of a personnel to undertake the actual work. Hitherto, the technical men who have given attention to oil shale have been mining engineers, chemists, or others from allied fields who have studied the subject themselves. In the future, however, men must be trained for oil shale work as a specialty. The need is recognized by the Colorado School of Mines and is being provided for."[51]

During the 1920-25 period, at least four companies erected retorts at the Colorado School of Mines. The purpose of such actions is not entirely clear, but may have been only for testing the retorts. In any event, in 1920, it was reported that:

"At the Colorado School of Mines two retorts, each of commercial size, are under construction. A Stalman retort by the General Petroleum Company of Kansas City; and a Wallace retort by George W. Wallace, of East St. Louis, Illinois. On the completion of these retorts, the Colorado School of Mines will be prepared to make complete retorting tests on oil shale in commercial quantities."[52]

In 1919-20 J. H. Ginet tested a retort at the Colorado School of Mines prior to its being moved and erected on the property of The Monarch Shale Oil Company on Conn Creek, north of De Beque, Colorado. A description of this retort and its operation is included under the section of this book describing the operations of The Monarch Shale Oil Company.

A 1925 publication reported that the Porter Process Company, Denver, Colorado, had an experimental plant in the Powerhouse of the Colorado School of Mines. The retorting process (Fig 18) was described as follows:

"The Porter 50-ton retort is of the oval-vertical type and is 1 ft. in diameter and 15 ft. in height. Oil shale, in 1-in. pieces, is moved through it by gravity and agitation, and steam is used to produce ammonia in the lower part of the retort. Water-gas made from spent shale is used as fuel and is burned at the bottom of the retort. The retort is divided into four different heat zones, in each of which there is a stirring device. In the upper zones, the heat is not allowed to exceed 700°F., while in the two lower sections the temperature is increased to 1000°-1200°F."[53]

Reports of tests made with these units are not evident in the literature researched, and the extent of testing and tests performed is not available.

Results of School of Mines tests on oil shales which had been reported to contain precious metals are cited elsewhere in this report.

It is assumed that the retorts and testing facilities cited were dismantled by 1930 when interest in oil shale had all but disappeared.

Champion Oil Shale & Refining Company

This company was organized by a group of Las Vegas, New Mexico, businessmen.

Organized   : September 18, 1919—State
                        of New Mexico
Capitalized   : $4,000,000 par value $2.00
President   : W. C. Sanders
Vice-President : J. A. Wilson

Fig. 18—The Porter continuous oil shale eduction and refining process plant at the Colorado School of Mines, Golden, Colorado. (From The Shale Review, *November, 1920.)*

Secretary	:	C. B. Wheeler
Treasurer	:	C. U. Strong
Location	:	Near Rulison Station—6 miles from Grand Valley
Property	:	640 acres shale & 80 acres plant site
Plant	:	No retort
Mine	:	None
Production	:	None

The Shale Review of August 1920 stated:

"Champion Company will build a Brown type retort. The Champion Oil Shale and Refining Company, whose principal place of business is at East Las Vegas, New Mexico, announced to its stockholders that it has made a contract for the immediate installation of retorts on its property in Garfield County, Colorado. This contract calls for the completion of the plant in 90 days, and shares of the Company which have heretofore been sold at their par value of $1, have been advanced in price to $2. It is understood that the contract mentioned has been made with H. F. Brown of Newark, N.J., who has recently inspected the shale field and has devised a process for shale treatment which looks feasible. The proposed plant will have a capacity of 300 tons daily."

Then in November 1920, *The Shale Review* reported:

"The Champion Oil Shale & Refining Company of East Las Vegas, New Mexico, will be merged with the Index Oil Shale Company of Denver. It owns shale deposits in the De Beque district."

Prior to this merger, Champion Company had constructed trails and roads on its property.

The company was dissolved on November 29, 1920. It had neither built a retort nor mined any oil shale.

Colorado Carbon Company

The Colorado Carbon Company was one of the first companies to be formed to work oil shales in Colorado.

Organized	:	November 18, 1915
Capitalized	:	$50,000 or 1000 shares at $50.00 each
President	:	T. E. Stevens
Vice-President	:	G. W. Holdrege
Secretary	:	Richard E. Leach
Location	:	Kimball Creek, 27 miles from De Beque, Colorado

Property	:	30 claims, 12 of which are patented
Plant	:	Operated two retorts, one a German retort in Kansas City, Missouri, in 1916 and a Thompson or Colorado Carbon retort built in Denver in 1921. There was no retort on the oil shale claims
Mine	:	Open cut
Production	:	Reported 70 barrels from 35 tons of shale in 1920-21.[54] No record of other production. [The obtaining of 70 barrels of oil from 35 tons of shale is questioned since this would require 100% recovery from 84 gal/ton shale. This does not seem reasonable or possible.]

In 1916, the company purchased a one-half mile cable tramway and towers. It had three substantial cabins and had constructed trails to the top of the mesa where the shale beds outcropped. It is doubtful if the tramway ever was erected. Spools of cable (Fig 19) were observed on the property by the author but there was no evidence of tower foundations or other remains. The Colorado Bureau of Mines report for 1921 notes that small lots of shale were shipped to states and manufacturers, but few other details were given. The report, however, does state that 70 barrels of oil were produced from 35 tons of shale. This must have taken place in the retort located in Denver. *The Petroleum Times* of March 26, 1921, states:

"Colorado Carbon Company retort. The retort installed in the old Neff Brewery building in Denver by the Colorado Carbon Company consists of a specially constructed iron tube about 25 feet long and a foot in diameter set horizontally in a brick oven. Heat is supplied by a series of gas burners arranged beneath the retort. Finely ground shale is fed continuously into one end of the tube from a hopper and carried slowly through the retort by a screw conveyor, being subjected to increasing temperatures as it proceeds through the tube. Three pipes penetrating the top of the retort tube one near each end and the other near the middle, provide exits for the vapours formed in the distillation of the shale. Those vapors produced in the cooler parts of the retort near the point where the shale enters, are taken to air and water cooled condensers, but those made in hotter parts of the retort and taken off through the other two pipes are returned into the retort near the cool end and subjected to reheating and cracking.''

Mr. W. R. Lewis, M.A., reported the following in his article, ''Seeing the Shale Fields'', which was published in the September 1920 issue of *The Mountain States Mineral Age*:

''A most interesting classification of Kimball Creek Shales has been made by Lewis W. Leach, an experienced chemist and engineer who has been in the field since 1915. Mr. Leach first came to the district in search of a 'Wurtzilite' shale and a 'Fishegg' shale, varieties which he had seen in Austria and which the Germans have found so very commercial in the manufacture of coal tar drugs and dye products. These he is said to have found in the most satisfactory deposits on Kimball Top, near the head of Kimball Creek. We will name briefly the twenty-two varieties as outlined and shown us by Mr. Leach.

Fig. 19—Colorado Carbon Company's plant site showing one of several spools of tramway cable, never installed. (1967 *photograph by author.*)

1. Wurtzilite Black Shale—Massive, bearing coal tar drugs.
2. Stratified Black—Rich, fractures break horizontally.
3. Curly Black—Very rich, fractures in curly shape, bears enamels, varnishes and lacquers.
4. Sandstone shale—Outcropping shows blue color, sand strata mixed with shale, both bearing oil.
5. Mineralized Black—with streaks of mineral matter, yielding glass and allied minerals.
6. Common Black—the most common commercial variety.
7. Iron Black—bearing flakes of iron pyrites, small amount of gold.
8. Paper Black—under massive black, yields hydrocarbone at low temperatures; easily worked.
9. Streaked Black—iron gray, seams of pyrite.
10. Zinc Gray Oxide—sometimes yielding 150 pounds of zinc per ton.
11. Zinc White Sulphide—zinc shows in pin points.
12. Mineralized Gray—bearing Bezol and Picric acid.
13. Common Gray—low oil content, horizontal fractures.
14. Streaked Gray—similar to common gray.
15. Lead Gray—bearing about thirty-five gallons oil per ton and some lead, zinc and silver.
16. Gray Antimony—very heavy, yields antimony, occurs in seams between the strata black.
17. Silver Gray—highest elevation, resembles iron gray; carries a little silver and traces of cobalt.
18. Ribbon Shale—mixed with sandstone occurring at highest altitudes.
19. Waxy Paraffine Brown—fracture like paper shale, fifteen to twenty percent paraffin.
20. Curly Brown—less oil than curly black, same fracture.
21. Mineralized Gray—similar to streaked gray but sandstone mineralized.
22. A New Mineralized Gray—not yet analyzed.

"Mr. Leach considers the Wurtzilite the most valuable formation, declaring it to be made up of Wedgerite, containing icthyol, gramahite, for rubber compounding and the Wurtzilite rich in acids and chemicals. He states that he has a deposit of fossilized fisheggs fifty feet in depth and of large dimensions."

Mr. Charles L. Jones in his October 1920 *Mellon Institute Report* stated: "...I believe the Company [Colorado Carbon Co.] to have good backing. While Mr. Leach is impractical to an almost humorous degree, and fools himself rather seriously, he probably would not be left in charge if large operations were started."

The Colorado Bureau of Mines report for 1922 mentions the bucket tram and development work, but no production. The 1923 report shows 15 men employed most of the year, but again no record of production. No further evidence of activity was found in the literature, and no mention of dissolution of the company was noted. It is assumed the claims were abandoned along with the Denver retort.

Columbia Oil Shale and Refining Company

The land holdings of this company were transferred to the Dow Chemical Corporation in 1955.

Organized	:	November 23, 1917
Capitalized	:	$10 million, 300,000 shares preferred, 700,000 common stock
President	:	William B. Hall
Vice-President	:	Unknown
Secretary	:	David A. Shepard
Agent	:	F. A. Goodale
Property	:	About 6000 acres
Location	:	East Middle Fork of Parachute Creek
Plant	:	No retort. Good camp, hydroelectric plant
Mine	:	An adit about 25 feet in length and open cuts
Production	:	None

The Columbia Oil Shale and Refining Company acquired rights to its oil shale claims after they had been located by others. Because this land-exchange occurred when interest in oil shale was high it is assumed that a high price was paid for the land.[55]

A good camp was constructed with needed roads and trails. A small hydroelectric plant was installed and the electricity was used to operate an electric auger drill. A small adit was driven to a depth of 20–25 feet into the outcrop. The electric auger drill apparently overheated easily and open-cut mining replaced the adit operation after 1921.[56]

Reports to the Colorado Bureau of Mines showed that in 1921 a 23-foot tunnel (adit) was driven, a hydroelectric plant was erected, trails and open cuts were constructed and a work force of 4 men was employed. The 1922 report showed that 5 to 15 men were engaged in assessment work and in road and trail work. The 1923 report showed assessment work and open cuts. No shale was reported shipped, nor was any production of oil reported.

The Columbia Oil Shale and Refining Company property was deeded to the Dow Chemical Company in August of 1955. Some 48 claims, many patented, totaling about 5800 acres, were involved in this transaction.[57]

No reports of activities on the Columbia property were noted after 1923.

Continental Oil Shale Mining and Refining Company

Organized	:	Incorporated August 19, 1919, State of Colorado. Dissolved October 28, 1919, State of Colorado. Incorporated November 22, 1919, State of Arizona
Capitalized	:	$2,500,000—10,000,000 shares at 25 cents per share. (Advertisements offered stock for 1 cent per share)
President	:	E. L. Krushnic
Vice-President	:	J. A. Payne
Secretary	:	E. M. Becker
Property	:	Claimed 3,500 to over 6,000 acres at various times
Location	:	Rio Blanco County, Colorado, 15–17 miles northwest of Rifle, Colorado, on upper Piceance Creek
Plant	:	50 ton-per-day retort on site
Mine	:	One adit 5 ft. by 5.5 ft. by 9 ft. deep and small open cuts on outcrop
Production	:	Very small amounts of oil produced

Mr. E. L. Krushnic, President of Continental Oil Shale Mining and Refining Company, had been an editor of a magazine devoted to petroleum until he learned about oil shale from Dr. A. R. Bailey. Continental obtained its mining claims from Dr. Bailey by merger with the Oil Development Company, one of Dr. Bailey's companies. Bailey was a major stockholder in Continental.[58] Figure 20 is a copy of an advertisement for sale of Continental stock. Figure 21 is a view of the retort.

The Shale Review of December 1920 described the early efforts of this company as follows:

"... Continental Oil Shale Mining and Refining Company was organized in November, 1918. Its preliminary financial arrangements were so suc-

cessful as to permit the placing of an order for the first unit of the retorting plant in May, 1919. Design, manufacture and construction of this retort was under the direction of Hartley & Dormann, mechanical engineers of Denver, the contract for the shop work being placed with the Plains Iron Works Company. Erection was completed and the first trial run made December 1, 1919. It was stated that in spite of the adverse weather conditions, two feet of snow on the ground, the first run was satisfactory in every respect.

"In designing this retort, a careful study of all available literature on the subject was made and the very best points selected, the whole being incorporated into a consistent design and packed at every point by sound and recognized engineering principles. Particular attention was paid in the general design of the installation to economy of operation. The development carried on during the summer of 1920 has definitely proven that the operation of this retort is as near automatic as is possible to make equipment lacking the human brain.

"With the opening of the weather early in 1920, a series of experimental runs, covering trials of different fuels, trials for efficiency and the like, were carried on with the retort and its high value definitely established under actual operation conditions."

At least double the verbiage presented here is in the original article, and praise for the retort, the stockholders and company officials is plentiful. However, nowhere does the article mention that oil was produced or disposed of in any way.

The Colorado Continuous retort, so highly praised in *The Shale Review* was described by W. A. Hamor[59] as follows:

"The Colorado continuous retort (capacity, 25 to 40 tons per 24 hours) consists of a vertical castiron chamber, 2 ft. in diameter and 22 ft. high, set in a brick furnace. The oil shale, crushed to ½-in. size, is fed from a hopper into the retort at the top and is lowered by a helical conveyor, which regulates the speed with which it passes through the distillation zone (temperature 1000°F). The vapors are withdrawn from the retort through a number of pipes at different elevations and carried through large air- and water-cooled condensers. Oil and the uncondensible gases are burned to supply heat for the retorting. The spent

WHY DRILL FOR OIL? WE HAVE MOUNTAINS OF IT!

1 Cent a share **No Well to Drill—No Dry Holes—No Expensive Machinery** 1 Cent a share

The Continental Oil Shale Mining & Refining Company, an oil shale corporation that has had the pick of the richest shale lands, organized by men who have investigated and have made a study of the shale possibilities.

GET IN ON THE GROUND FLOOR OF THIS ENTERPRISE

The authorized report of the U. S. Geological Society has endorsed the shale industry and has pronounced it as one of the greatest undeveloped resources in America.

The oil shale will produce over a hundred commercial products, various chemicals which are the basis of dyestuffs, ammonia, creosote, mineral rubber now being used in tires, manufacturing paint, roofing, etc.

In response to the many inquiries and questions asked us we wish to herewith enlighten you. It is doubtful if any oil shale enterprise ever started business with better properties, a more capable management, a more comprehensive policy and more favorable prospects than the Continental Oil Shale Mining and Refining Company.

The possibilities of this company are so great as to be almost unlimited, it would take the life time of several generations and a refinery of a thousand tons a day capacity to exhaust the shale deposits on our property (4,800 acres). This company owns its land, does not lease or have to pay rentals or royalties.

We feel that the shale industry is going to be one of the biggest industries in Colorado and that this company will be a factor of great importance.

It is the purpose of this company to create an industry of vast magnitude for the production, refining and marketing, gasoline, high grade lubricating oils and the various by products. We want to start building and to continue to add units until we have one of the largest and most profitable business enterprises in the state of Colorado.

That is why we are urging you to come in on the ground floor, that is the reason why we are offering the first block of stock at this ridiculously low price, one cent a share, and this stock is forever non-assessable.

Remember the price of this stock will advance as soon as the first block is subscribed for and will continue to advance as we progress with the financing of the company. We desire that you investigate our company, realizing when you investigate you will subscribe for a large block of the stock.

Remember this—now is the time to become a stockholder while the price is a ground floor one.

WHY THE SHALE INDUSTRY APPEALS TO OIL MEN

The fact of the whole proposition is, the value will not be temporary, but a lasting and permanent investment. There is sufficient oil shale on our holdings to last the life time of several generations and the oil is in the shale. No uncertainty of drilling oil wells, no dry holes, no water holes, no settling of production, or drowning out of oil wells, which causes the bottom to drop out of your stocks. No spending of a large treasury reserve, or your profits from one good lease, in drilling dry holes or crooked holes, or looking for new production after you have pumped your well dry of oil.

THE PURPOSE OF THE COMPANY

is to develop its holdings as fast as possible by selling an interest in these holdings in the form of stock to the investor who is looking for a good investment. Every acre of our holdings has rich oil shale. The ledge that runs for ten to two hundred feet in thickness will yield from thirty to ninety gallons of oil per ton. It is impossible to even guess at the millions of barrels of oil that our 4,800 acres contain.

The Continental Oil Shale Mining & Refining Company presents this opportunity to participate in the profits of the future by supplying part of the finances to build a 250 ton refinery.

OUR PROPERTY

The shale ledge on our property is a continuation of the U. S. Government Mammoth Naval Reserve.

4800 ACRES

The 4,800 acres of The Continental Oil Shale Mining and Refining Company's property consists of 30 full mining claims, designated, known, located and recorded as "Colloid Claims" numbered from 1 to 24 inclusive; "Hydrock Claims," Nos. 6, 7, 8, and 24, and "Petrolite Claims," Nos. 11 and 13, located in Township 3 South, Range 94 and 95, West of the Sixth Principal Meridian, Rio Blanco County, State of Colorado, all of which said Placer Claims are more particularly described in the location notices which are of record in the office of the Clerk and Recorder of the said Rio Blanco County in the State of Colorado.

THE COMPANY'S OBJECTIVE

is to purchase and install retorts and a refinery and immediately begin operations on as large a scale as its finances will permit. As soon as the first unit of the refinery is installed work will begin and more units will be added as fast as possible.

It is the plan of the Continental Oil Shale Mining and Refining Co. to make this concern the largest of its kind in the United States, as we have the richest oil shale on our property in the world.

The Continental Oil Shale Mining and Refining Co.

Principal Offices
Fourth Floor Gas & Electric Bldg., Denver, Colo.

Incorporated — Capital $2,500,000
Par Value 25 Cents a Share—Forever Non-Assessable.

OFFICERS AND DIRECTORS

E. L. KRUSHNIC, President, Oil Man. K. M. BECKER, Secretary, Connected with a National Bank. J. A. PAYNE, Vice President, President Great Western Publishing Co. WHEELER S. PECK, Deputy City Clerk. FRED F. VIDEON, Buyer for the J. S. Brown Mercantile Co.

DEPOSITORY, INTERSTATE TRUST COMPANY

CUT OUT THIS COUPON, SEND IN YOUR SUBSCRIPTION, TODAY

THE CONTINENTAL OIL SHALE MINING AND REFINING COMPANY
Fourth Floor Gas & Electric Building, Denver, Colorado.

Gentlemen:

Find inclosed $..............for................shares of stock of the Continental Oil Shale Mining and Refining Company, same being absolutely and forever non-assessable at........cents per share.

Name ....2..

Town ....State ....

You may pay one-fourth down, balance in three equal monthly payments, stock certificate will be forwarded upon completion of payments.

Address all communications and make all checks and money orders payable to the company. No cash order accepted for less than 500 shares. No partial payment orders accepted for less than 1,000 shares.

All mail orders will be filled at the present price.

We reserve the right to refund your money in the event present allotment of stock is oversubscribed.

MANAGEMENT OF THE COMPANY

The management is composed of men active in the business affairs of Colorado, whose integrity is beyond question. The method and proposition they offer to the investor is a fair one and above criticism.

They are offering the stock purchaser an opportunity to come in on equitable basis and assist in development.

OFFICERS AND DIRECTORS

There are no salaried officers and no fabulous commissions are paid to agents of the Continental Oil Shale Mining and Refining Co. The officers and directors have invested cash and time in this project, and are men of integrity and keen business sagacity.

The Continental Oil Shale Mining and Refining Company is not being promoted to make money out of selling stock, but the organizers, knowing the great wealth of oil and by-products on this property, and also believing that the public will at once recognize the merits of this stock as an investment, will be glad to purchase the stock to help develop their holdings and thereby share in the profits.

Fig. 20—Promotional advertisement for the Continental Oil Shale Mining and Refining Company. (From The Shale Review, *1920.)*

Fig. 21—*Continental Oil Shale Mining and Refining Company's plant. Taken in mid-winter when first test runs were made.* (*From* The Shale Review, *December,* 1920.)

shale is removed by a mechanical device, through a water-seal at the bottom of the retort." [This is the fractional eduction concept later proved to be essentially invalid].

In addition to the retort, the plant site also contained a bunk house, a cabin, a blacksmith shop and a crusher. A mineral examiner of the day estimated the total cost of this plant (Fig 22) at $15,000.[60] The

records researched do not include mention of any production-type runs of the retort. The spent shale pile on the site when first examined about 20 years ago indicated very little operation. This plant, as was the case with many of the early oil shale plants, used tar sands for some of its trial runs.

The influence of Dr. A. R. Bailey on the operations of the Continental Company are probably impossible

Fig. 22—*View of Continental Oil Shale Mining and Refining Company's plant. May* 1920. (*From* The Shale Review, *May,* 1920.)

to assess at this date. However, while the Continental Oil Shale stock was offered to the public[61] (as low as 1¢ per share), it also was offered to purchasers of twenty acres of mining claims under Dr. A. R. Bailey's promotion. The promotion also included a lease form in favor of the company to induce the purchaser to believe that the company would develop the property.[62]

An Inspector's Report, General Land Office, Glenwood Springs, Colorado, March 19, 1926, stated:

"The Continental Oil Shale Mining and Refining Company was a subsidiary company organized by Dr. A. R. Bailey to assist him in his scheme of selling placer locations. This company put up a small retort on the SE¼NW¼ Sec. 6, T4S, R94W. It was run for a few hours and a little oil distilled from the oil shale. The Continental Oil Shale Mining and Refining Company has decided to abandon its claims and no assessment work was performed for the years ending July 1, 1923, up to July 1, 1925."

No records of oil production were reported to, or by, the Colorado Bureau of Mines. The company was dissolved in October 1927. Figure 23 shows the plant site as it appeared in 1978.

The Grand Valley Oil & Shale Co. (Consumers Oil and Shale Company of Chicago)

This was an Arizona Corporation owning oil lands and having shale holdings in addition.

Organized	:	About 1918 or 1919
Capitalized	:	$250,000
President	:	Ralph R. Lagley

*Fig. 23—View of plant site, Continental Oil Shale Mining and Refining
Company, 1978. (Photograph by author.)*

Vice-President   : J. R. Rubey
Secretary-Treasurer : W. A. Rule
Property   : Amount unknown
Location   : On Starkey Gulch
                       about 6 miles from
                       Grand Valley
Plant   : Plant site on prop-
                       erty—stone quarried
                       but no construction
Mine   : None
Production   : None

Dean Winchester, U.S. Geological Survey, in his
May 1921 addition to his earlier *Manuscript on Oil
Shale of the Rocky Mountain Region* reported:

> "The Grand Valley Oil & Shale Co. during 1920
> constructed an automobile road from Parachute
> Creek up Starkey Gulch to its plant site 6 miles
> northwest of Grand Valley and were laying foun-
> dations for the installation of a Stalmann retort-
> ing plant."

The only substantiating information appeared in
the *Mountain States Mineral Age* of September 1920
which stated that: "The Grand Valley Shale Oil Co.,
now having built a large Stalmann process, 150 tons
capacity . . ." There was no additional information.

No retort was built nor were any components of a
retort apparently ever on this site. Validation of
published information regarding oil shale was very
poor, and this report of a retort is typical.

The author's visit to this site confirms that a road
was constructed up Starkey Gulch that required
several bridges. The bridges had washed out long ago
and access was only by walking and picking one's own
pathway. The road evidently ended at a small 100–150
foot hill. A surface tramway had been constructed
from the road to the top of the hill (Fig 24). A portion
of the hilltop had been leveled, apparently for use as a
plant site. Several tons of flat sandstone rocks of irregular size and shape were stacked in the leveled area
(Fig 25). There was no sign that actual construction of
any kind had ever taken place. There was no evidence
of trails from the plant site to the oil shale outcrops.
There were no dumps, no tramway and no signs of
mining or retorting.

References to this company or companies were not
located in the literature after 1921.

Fig. 24—Remains of surface tramway from road to plant, site of the Grand Valley Oil & Shale Company. (1967 photograph by author.)

Index Oil Shale Company

Organized	:	Incorporated October 1920 —State of Colorado
Capitalized	:	$1,000,000 par value $1.00 per share
President	:	Chester W. Church
Vice-President	:	Wm. T. Mack
Secretary	:	E. B. Wheeler
Property	:	640 acres near Mt. Blaine, 640 acres near Rulison Station
Location	:	Mt. Blaine, about 12 miles northwest of De Beque
Plant	:	Brown retort and probably the largest camp and associated facilities of any of the 1920 oil shale operations in Colorado
Mine	:	Short 60 foot tunnel plus open cut operations
Production	:	Small production from limited operations

Fig. 25—Plant site of Grand Valley Oil & Shale Company showing quarried stone for retort construction. (1967 photograph by author.)

The Index Oil Shale Company operation is essentially the story of Harry L. Brown. Brown was the inventor of the "Brown" retort used. He was the principal stockholder and personally loaned to the company most of its operating funds. He was a former employee of the American Chicle Company of New Jersey. Brown and his associates originally were interested in selling retorts rather than in operating them. (The Brown Process was the property of a corporation known as the Shale Oil Machinery and Supply Company, of which C. W. Church was president.)[63] They contracted to build a retort for the Mt. Blaine Oil Shale Company, but that company was unable to raise the money to pay for the retort. A supplemental arrangement was made whereby Index received sixteen claims of the Mt. Blaine Company and started construction of a plant using the Brown retort.[64]

Index started building its plant in July 1920. The retort was completed in November 1920, but the plant still was being erected by April 1921. In November 1921 the first test runs were made. Plant construction and modifications continued throughout its existence and was never reported as "completed."[65] The plant was a large one, probably the largest of all 1920 era oil shale

plants in Colorado (Fig 26) and consisted of at least the following:

"One large and two small bunkhouses, a mess hall, cookhouse, carpenter shop, blacksmith shop, a small office building, a laboratory and a garage, all of wooden frames covered with tarpaper. There were two crushers, three storage bins, two eighty-horsepower boilers, a ninety-horsepower steam engine, a 2600 foot tramway and storage tanks (50,000 gal. total capacity). Later condensing equipment consisting of reciprocating stills, a compressor, and a condensor box were added." [A complete inventory of the plant was recited in a receivership proceeding].[66]

The Brown retort (Fig 27), heart of the operation, was described in the November 17, 1924, *Chemical and Metallurgical Engineering Magazine* as follows:

"The retort used by the Index Company was designed by H. L. Brown, of Glen Ridge, N.J. It is a horizontal, rotary type and consists of three tubes, 30 in. in diameter and 20 ft. long, made of 3/8-inch steel. Inside of each tube is a helical fin, 4 in. wide with a 2-ft. pitch on its inside periphery. As the retort revolves the fin serves to advance the shale 2 ft. with each revolution. The tubes are

Fig. 26—View of Index Oil Shale Company's plant near De Beque, Colorado, as it appeared in early 1920s. (From Oil Shale, Ralph McKee, 1925.)

Fig. 27—Brown process retort of the Index Oil Shale Company, near De Beque, Colorado. (From The Shale Review, April, 1922.)

joined in the same axis by two stuffing boxes, at which points there are offtakes for the vapors as well as connections for the entry of superheated steam. The ends of the tubes are closed with castings that hold the automatic seals for charging the raw shale and discharging the spent material. The main outlet for the vapors is also at the end of the retort.

"Each tube of the retort is surrounded by a furnace of special design and heated individually by oil burners directed tangentially at the top of the retort. The upper part of each furnace consists of ten removable sections. The furnace is lined with firebrick and Sil-O-Cel insulating brick. The various sections of the retort are turned separately by gears which are belt driven from a countershaft.

"The crushed shale from a large bin beneath the crusher passes down a chute to the charging end of the retort, where an automatic push feed forces it into the retort, which is rotated at about 5 r.p.m. The furnace is held at a temperature of around 1,100 deg. F., but the extreme heat of the vapors at the outlet is only 550 deg. F. The spent shale was to be removed by a mechanical conveyor and wasted over the sloping hillside in front of the plant.

"At the time the plant was constructed it was doubtless believed that considerable fractionation of vapors would result from the three separate offtakes for the gases. Operation showed, however, that by far the greatest volume of gas was taken from the outlet at the end of the retort . . ."

This same article also states:

". . .The rated capacity of the plant was 400 tons per 24 hours, but the test runs made during November, 1922, indicated that the retort worked most efficiently when the feed was at the rate of 4 tons per hour, or roughly 100 tons per day."

The plant was run only intermittently. Inspectors' reports of the Colorado Bureau of Mines are indicative of activities as are items published in the literature of the day. These sources report the following:

1921—*The Shale Review,* April and July issues: . . . plant "not completed yet".
Colorado Bureau of Mines: ". . . mining in open cuts."

1922—*The Shale Review,* February: "No runs since last fall when condensing units were found to be defective. New ones being con-structed a cost of $30,000." March issue reports "a special excursion of eastern visitors and that test runs were made nearly every day. Moving pictures were taken with reels sent to England."[67] April issue reports "oil sands from Gallup, New Mexico were satisfactorily tested.[68]
Colorado Bureau of Mines: "Work halted, lack of funds."

1923—Colorado Bureau of Mines: "12 men employed. Small amounts of gasoline, produced by a retort run by electric power during a short operation in 1922, was put on market in De Beque."

1924—Colorado Bureau of Mines, August: "No activity report."
De Beque News, December 1: ". . . large crusher being taken up the mountain [to mine area] . . . and [soon] will be ready . . . to supply retorting plant . . . new cable for tram received and being strung . . . not stretched and put into service . . . No definite time has been set for beginning regular operation."

1925—*De Beque News:* "Prospects bright for resumption of operations by Index Shale Oil Co."

1926—Colorado Bureau of Mines, June: "4 men employed at plant."

1927—Colorado Bureau of Mines, November: "5 men employed at plant, 3 at mine; Occasional use of tram to transport shale; No production; No shipments except samples."

1928—Company went into receivership. Figure 28 shows the plant area in 1967.

The capability of the Brown retort was questioned very early. In 1922, Lewis B. Skinner, Manager of the Research Department of the Midwest Refining Company said: [69]

"With respect to your query as to whether I have followed the activities of the Index Oil Shale Co., I should advise that I had occasion to pass upon this device put out by Mr. Brown and reported adversely.

". . . This immature design was decided by him (Brown) in spite of the fact that our western country is full of revolving tube designs, which have been used in the ore reduction business, all of which have been developed by competent engineers with the idea of eliminating lost time for shutdowns and repair."

W. H. Hoffman looked at this plant for the Texas

Fig. 28—Index Oil Shale Company's plant site as it appeared in 1967. (*Photograph by author.*)

Company in 1929 and reported:

"The equipment is out of balance and the plant has been erected according to the ideas of the inventor with little or no regard to the fundamental principles governing the destructive distillation of solids. Commercial operation has never been attempted and specific claims made as to value of various products without sufficient data to justify this expansion and these assertions."

Others also were on record questioning the previous technological experience of Mr. Brown. As was the case in other oil shale operations, the mining of the oil shale seemed to be a minor problem.

"In its early operation [Index Oil Shale Co.] it was planned to utilize the rich shale that could be easily obtained by shooting down the exposed faces or escarpments on Mount Blaine, a thousand or more feet above the plant site. This shale was run into a natural chute down the slope to a bulkhead, from which it was hauled 1,800 ft. to the crushing plant. When operations are resumed, it is planned to build a surface tram from the bulkhead that will connect directly with the hopper above the crusher."[70]

A tramway was installed in late 1924, but a lack of records of production indicate that its use was very limited prior to 1928 when the company went into receivership. Figure 29 shows the trail to the mine.

Brown stated that about $250,000 was spent on the plant and $135,000 was added in the building of an absorption plant.[71]

The most active individual in this corporation was Harry L. Brown. He owned 191,986 shares of the 912,000 shares outstanding, and he had loaned $144,464.30 of the company's $273,843.03 total debt. Other major investors were associates of Brown from the eastern United States.[72] The corporation had no earnings. It was financed partly through sale of stock and loans from stockholders.[73]

The company became short of funds by late 1922, and a lien was filed against its property in December 1922. This lien was released early in 1923, but the company was again in financial difficulty by mid-1923. At least seven different liens were filed on the company's land during 1923. In 1928 the company went into receivership. By 1930 Index was defunct and inactive.[74]

Thus, this plant started construction in July 1920 and conducted its first test run in November 1921. The company operated on an irregular basis until 1927. During this time there was no reported production other than a Colorado Bureau of Mines report that a "small amount of gasoline, produced by a retort run by electric power during a short operation in 1922, was put on the market in De Beque." Small amounts of shale oil produced during demonstration and experimental operations were not reported to the Colorado Bureau of Mines or to the public, thus the amounts must have been very limited. This assessment

is believed to be true in spite of the article "A Look at Oil Shale in Colorado", by J. D. Freeman, in the February 1964 issue of the *Rocky Mountain Oil Reporter*[75] that contained the following:

"The Brown Process plant had never run more than a few hours continuously. Over a jug of peach brandy one night, we pledged that within five days we would have things set to make a ten-day continuous run of 100 tons each 24 hours. By golly we did it! There was shale oil, ammoniacal liquor, and spent shale all over that hillside along with some four feet of snow. The laboratory had plenty of material to play with."

The date that this ten-day run occurred is not clear, but it appears to have been prior to April 1923. A ten-day run of 100 tons per day, assuming a 25-gallon-per-ton recovery of oil, would have produced 25,000 gallons of oil or about 600 barrels. There is nothing in the literature of the day or in the reports of the Colorado Bureau of Mines to support this claim. Available production records do not credit this amount of production to all of the oil shale operations of Colorado during the years from 1917 to 1925.

Fig. 29—Trail from Index Oil Shale Company's plant to location of oil shale deposits. (1967 photograph by author.)

Mr. Freeman's article also contained the following: "Several thousand tons of this spent shale was picked up and hauled away from where it was left at the Index Plant on Mount Blaine. This plant was between Clear and Roan Creeks, 18 miles north of De Beque. Most of the spent shale was used in peach orchards around Palisade. It was found to be a sure cure for "yellow" trees, and it improved the qualities of the fruit wherever it was used."

The availability of "several thousand tons" of spent shale at the Index site is not substantiated by any records of the day.

Index Oil Shale Company may have had adequate financing to develop a retort for commercial production of shale oil; however, technology and know-how apparently were lacking. Although some stock was sold, it was not a stock promotion operation, but only another early-day effort that was not successful.

The Lackawanna Oil Shale Products Company

The Lackawanna was a public stock company.

Organized	:	October 11, 1917—State of Wyoming
Capitalized	:	Originally $1,000,000 at $1.00 per share—Raised to $5,000,000 at $5.00 per share
President	:	John Gaffy
Vice-President		John S. McCarthy
Secretary	:	John M. Keenan
Treasurer	:	Joseph W. Latham
Location	:	Conn Creek area, 12 miles north of De Beque
Property	:	1280 acres
Plant	:	Some shale was shipped and treated in a "Wallace" retort in St. Louis, Missouri, during 1919. In 1920, company advertisements stated a "Scott" retort was intended for use. Later it was announced a "Randall" retort was selected. There never was a retort on the property in Colorado
Mine	:	None. Assessment work only
Production	:	None

This company proposed to erect a plant of 1000 tons daily capacity and expand to 2000 tons per day. A refinery also was proposed to be built near De Beque plus a pipe line to the retorting area.

With the decision to use a "Randall" retort (Fig 30), construction was started in June 1920 at Wilkes-Barre, Pennsylvania. This retort was described in the September 1920 issue of *The Shale Review* as follows:

"The Lackawanna Oil Shale Products Company announced that its retort on which construction was begun in June is now being made ready for shipment. The retort is being constructed by the Vulcan Iron Works of Wilkesbarre, Pa. The retort is the invention of J. W. Randall, a New York engineer, and is of the continuous type. Some idea of its mammoth size may be gained from its shipping weight, 244,700 pounds. It is a circular tube 110 feet long, and therefore, has a weight of over one ton per foot of length. In general it consisted of a long hollow cylinder, which lies horizontally

Fig. 30—Randall retort of The Lackawanna Oil Shale Products Company, constructed at Wilkes Barre, Pennsylvania. (From The Shale Review, *February, 1921.)*

and is revolved over gas burners . . . Randall retorts have been used on a commercial scale for the manufacture of acetone, acetic acid, wood alcohol and similar products of destructive distillation. . . ."

The retort was never delivered to the property in Colorado.

The October 4, 1920, report of the Colorado Bureau of Mines said that six men were employed on the construction of roads and trails and that the Randall retort was expected in De Beque in 60 days. The January 1921 report stated that only assessment work was being done.

By 1921, liens had been filed against the assets of the company and the firm became inactive in Colorado in 1924.

The March Oil Shale Company

Organized	:	Incorporated August 30, 1917
Capitalized	:	$80,000 shares $1.00 each (Closed corporation)
President	:	C. A. Fisher
Vice-President	:	Unknown
Secretary	:	Ralph Hartzell
Property	:	2400 acres
Location	:	Wheeler Gulch
Plant	:	No retort. A camp, trails, tramway and foundations for equipment were constructed
Mine	:	A drift mine was started in 1920–21. No ore produced
Production	:	None

A syndicate of Denver men had been formed at the time of the oil excitement at Tisdale, Wyoming, for the purpose of procuring leases and other rights in oil lands. After a short campaign in Wyoming, Mr. C. A. Fisher, a syndicate member, suggested that the syndicate might do well if it interested itself in the oil shale business. Other syndicate members were favorable and, accordingly, Hartzell turned over to James Doyle approximately $1500 of unexpended company money to be used for location of oil shale claims.[76]

The March Oil Shale Company was incorporated. The mining claims were transferred to the corporation, and stock in the company was issued to each of the original members of the syndicate in proportion to his holdings in the syndicate. Shares also were given to two outsiders who helped locate the claims. The property was 3–4 miles north of Grand Valley in Wheeler Gulch.[77]

On September 17, 1920, a 20-year lease on the claims was granted to K. C. Schuyler, a syndicate member, with the provisions that he do the assessment work and pay a ten percent royalty. Later the agreement was changed to provide that Schuyler was to receive about 1,000 acres from the corporation when he had successfully operated an oil shale plant.[78]

Construction of facilities began in September 1920. Buildings and sheds were erected, a 4000–5000 foot surface tramway (Fig 31) was laid up the mountain to the oil shale, foundations (Fig 32 and Fig 33) for hoists and bins were built, and steam and electrical engines were installed.[79]

George Taff, working for, or in partnership with, Mr. Schuyler, designed a retort reported to be patterned after the Chew retort. No description was published of the Taff retort so no comparison can be made. The retort was manufactured in Wisconsin, but was never moved from there.[80]

On July 20, 1921, five men were killed in a tramway accident, and apparently little or no work was performed after that time.[81]

Colorado Bureau of Mines reports give a rough idea as to activities over several years.

> 1920—September 24 report: "Track tram equipment in Grand Valley to be about one mile in length."
>
> 1921—September 24 report: "13 men on property. Starting tunnel 8 ft. by 12 ft. Machinery on ground. Concrete foundations for hoist in and hoist being put in place."
>
> 1921—Report: "Roads, camp, etc. No oil, no shale produced. Works closed October 15, 1921."
>
> 1923—Report: "2400 acres. No shale produced. No oil produced. No work on plant."
>
> 1924—Report: "Actual operation not yet commenced."

In 1928, K. C. Schuyler released his interest in the mining claims to the corporation under his agreement. He had spent about $120,000 on the plant, and he sold most of his plant machinery for $10,000.[82]

The March Oil Shale Company did not sell stock nor did it erect a plant or produce any oil shale. The corporation became defunct and inactive on October 10, 1933.[83]

Fig. 31—Tramway cut at The March Oil Shale Company. Note shale cliffs in background and plant site in foreground. (1967 photograph by author.)

Fig. 32—Plant foundations of The March Oil Shale Company, Wheeler Gulch, near Grand Valley, Colorado. (1978 photograph by Robert L. Bolmer, Lakewood, Colorado.)

Fig. 33—Camp site and plant foundations, The March Oil Shale Company, near Grand Valley, Colorado. (1978 photograph by Robert L. Bolmer, Lakewood, Colorado.)

The Monarch Oil Shale Company

Organized	:	Incorporated October 4, 1919—State of Delaware
Capitalized	:	$10,000 at $0.01 per share
President	:	J. H. Ginet
Vice-President	:	Carle Whitehead
Secretary	:	J. B. Ginet
Property	:	240 acres
Location	:	Conn Creek about 12 miles northwest of De Beque
Plant	:	Ginet Retort—50 tons per day
Mine	:	Small underground mine
Production	:	About 75 barrels of oil

The plant (Figs 34, 35 and 36) was begun in the middle of 1920 and was completed by April 1921. Installation included a bunkhouse, office, surface tramway to the mine, improved roads and trails, gasoline motors, a crusher system and other equipment.[84]

The retort was a "Ginet retort" named after its inventor and president of the company. Joseph H. Ginet, who had been a Traveling Passenger Agent for the Missouri and Pacific Railway, and had a "mechanical turn of mind."[85] The retort was unusual in that it had been constructed to full size and tested in a building at the Colorado School of Mines for a year or two before the corporation started constructing its plant above De Beque.[86]

V. C. Alderson[87] described this operation as follows:

"The Monarch Oil Shale Company has erected a Ginet retort and has made nine test runs, the longest of which was for two days. Oil has been shipped in barrel lots for experimental use to the Calumet & Arizona Copper Company, the American Zinc Company, the Eagle Mining Company, and to Columbia University, New York. The retort is of the stationary horizontal type, twenty-five feet long, three feet in diameter and gas fired from below. The shale is advanced by an internal arrangement of revolving flanges or 'shovels'. The daily capacity of the retort is estimated at fifty tons. The vapors are taken off thru thirty-nine outlets at the top of the retort, are then combined and passed to the condensers. The shale is ground to one-half inch mesh and yields sixty-four gallons to the ton. The presence of water in the vapors is to be avoided by the installation of a preheater to evaporate, as far as possible, the moisture in the shale before the shale enters the retort proper. The shale stratum, 8 ft. thick, lies 1,000 feet above the retort. A tunnel seventy-five foot long has been driven into the shale bed with two twenty-foot drifts, one on either side of the tunnel. A four-inch pipe carries the shale from the crusher at the mouth of the tunnel, down to the retort."

C. L. Jones[88] of the Mellon Institute commented on this plant as follows:

"In the writer's opinion, the retort has no more and no less merit than any of the other proposed devices which agitate the shale in thin layers during distillation. In its present form, however, it is open criticism, in the inefficient arrangement of the burners, a very short path being provided for the flue gases, and also in the large ratio of vapor space to shale in the chamber, which would tend towards leaving oil vapors in the still for too long a period of time.

The *Railroad Red Book* for January 1922 reported the following:

"The Monarch Oil Shale Company has erected a Ginet retort at a cost of $103,700. The company has maintained a capable staff of chemists and engineers and is proceeding in a constructive manner. Hundreds of barrels of oil have been produced at a cost, according to the company at $1.42 a barrel, divided as follows: Mining 91 cents; crushing 10 cents; retorting 14 cents; and all other expenses 27 cents. The company is disposing of the crude oil for flotation purposes at $8.40 a barrel. Oil has been shipped in barrel lots for experimental use to the Calumet & Arizona Copper Company, the American Zinc Company, the Eagle Mining Company, and to Columbia University, New York."

In spite of the above, one barrel of oil ordered by Gulf Oil Company on May 23, 1921, was not delivered until February 11, 1922, even after several inquiries by Gulf asking for delivery.[89] The following reports of the Colorado Bureau of Mines help explain Gulf's problems in getting delivery.

1921—Report: "65 tons of shale mined, 71 barrels of oil produced."

1922—April 12 report (for year 1921): "10 operating periods; 1–29 hours, 9–2 hours each. [No oil production was reported. It is assumed the 71 barrels reported for 1921 were produced during these runs].

1923—January 9, report: "Retort plant not run to any extent."

Fig. 34—Completed Ginet retort of The Monarch Oil Shale Company near De Beque, Colorado. (From The Shale Review, *January,* 1921.)

Fig. 35—*Plant of The Monarch Oil Shale Company, north of De Beque,
Colorado.* (*From* The Shale Review, *April,* 1921).

Fig. 36—*Ginet retort of The Monarch Oil Shale Company, near De Beque,
Colorado.* (*From* The Shale Review, *August–September,* 1921.)

1924—August 25 and final report: "Plant not in operation. Experiments in refining shale oil being conducted."

1925—No report filed.

Monarch was a public stock company. Some extravagant statements were made, for example: "We expect to pay $1.00 per share in dividends each year, and probably more." ". . . the Government was behind it, there is absolutely no way to lose."[90]

The corporation attempted to sell a $50,000 bond issue (bonds carrying eight percent interest with a two-year maturity), but only about $8,500 of the issue were sold.[91] By April 1928 it was two years late in filing annual reports.

There is no evidence that the corporation was active after this time.[92]

In summary, the Monarch Oil Shale Company produced about 75 barrels of oil, mined and shipped about 2½ tons of oil shale to others, and shipped 25 barrels of shale oil to the City of Glenwood Springs, Colorado, to be used to surface streets, 10 or 12 barrels to Aspen, Colorado, 5 or 6 barrels to Memphis, 3 or 4 shipments of 1–3 barrels each to various mining concerns in Colorado, and 12 barrels to Mascot, Tennessee.[93]

Figure 37 shows the plant site in 1978.

The Mount Logan Oil Shale and Refining Company

Organized	:	June 29, 1917—State of Colorado
Capitalized	:	8,000–800,000 shares of stock at $0.01 each
President	:	T. A. Thompson
Vice-President	:	William Fitch
Secretary and General Manager	:	H. D. Locke
Treasurer	:	H. A. Quigley
Property	:	320 acres on Mount Logan
Plant	:	Three Galloupe retorts were found unsatisfactory and replaced by a Simplex retort in 1920
Mine	:	Underground mine and tramway
Production	:	52–70 barrels of oil and 2 or more carloads of mined shale shipped to others

The land and the plant site were about 4–6 miles north of De Beque, Colorado, on Mount Logan.

By March 1, 1918, the company had begun purchas-

Fig. 37—Site of The Monarch Oil Shale Company as it appeared in 1978. (Photograph by author.)

ing machinery for its plant; and by November 1918, it was erecting a plant in western Colorado. The first test runs were made after many delays on April 3, 1919.[94]

Three Galloupe retorts of a capacity of 20 tons per day each were erected by the company. These retorts had been constructed and tested at a foundry in Denver prior to shipment to De Beque.[95] By 1920 these retorts were found to be unsatisfactory,[96] and a fourth retort, called a Simplex retort (Fig 38) was built. The Simplex retort, of a capacity of 8-10 tons of shale per day was a modification of the Galloupe retort. It was described as being similar to an Edwards ore roaster.[97]

Dean Winchester[98] described this retort as follows:

"The single unit Simplex retort completed early in 1920 consists of an inclined hearth about 30 feet long and 3 feet wide constructed of cast iron. The retort chamber above the hearth is about 3 inches deep and its top is penetrated by five large take off pipes for the removal of vapors. Finely crushed shale is fed into the upper end of the retort by a screw conveyor and carried down across the hearth by the assistance of 15 geared agitators each of which scrapes the bottom of the retort moving in a circular direction. Spent shale is removed at the lower end of the retort through a shale seal. Crude oil is used in two burners located under the upper end of the hearth."

An article in the January 1921 issue of the *Railroad Red Book* describes the mine that supplied oil shale for the retorts as follows:

"At the mine of the Mount Logan Co., the shale beds are practically horizontal but outcrop in the cliffs of Mt. Logan about 3000 feet above the valley of Grand River [Colorado River] only about three miles away. Here the main entry has been driven more than 100 feet along the bed. A power-driven, auger drill is used to drill the holes for shooting down the shale and mining is by methods similar to those used in the winning of coal. The shale mined at this mine has been used by this and other companies in experimental work connected with the development of retorts for the distillation of the shale.

"The shale ore was delivered to the plant over a well-constructed, two-stage, mile-long, jig-back tramway. The Mt. Logan tram has been used to transport several hundred tons of shale from the company's mine to the retort site nearly 3,000 feet below."[99]

Figure 39 shows the plant and oil shale outcrop.

The auger drill referred to in the *Railroad Red Book*

article was described by J. L. Herwick in a 1921 letter to the editor of the *Grand Valley News*:

"Your correspondent, together with Mr. Joe Bellis, visited the Mount Logan oil shale plant on last Wednesday (1921) to witness the public demonstration that was being made with the company's new retort, and also with the new Cushman rotary drill they have lately perfected and installed at the shale mine.

"The drill is a wonder in every respect and so far surpasses any expectation that the writer had as to its ability. This drill is operated by a small gasoline engine and actually drilled several three- and four-foot holes two inches in diameter in six to seven minutes' time for each hole. We were told by the management that three men can break and deliver to the bin at the head of the tram 50 tons of shale per shift, and I must say you can readily believe the statement when you see the machine at work."

"An underground excavation provided living space at the mine for the miners; there was also a crusher, the start of a water cistern, and a loading terminal for the tramway."[100]

A Mr. Holmes, in October 1920, wrote a report for the Texas Company which described the plant:

"Aside from the retort the construction of this plant is so out of line that no importance could be placed upon the samples of oil as received from their condensers, as both vapor lines were so leaky that a large majority of the lighter products would escape into the atmosphere without being condensed."

The company had many problems. Its best and only year of operation was 1921 during which 52 barrels of oil were produced.[101] It had orders for 80 barrels of oil from an Apex Refinery,[102] but had so much trouble and delay in making the shale oil, the refinery was leased to another party.[103] They experienced similar problems in filling single barrel orders for a Luther Jones.[104]

A chronology of operations based upon reports of inspectors for the Colorado Bureau of Mines and items published in the literature of the day follows:

1919—Colorado Bureau of Mines. Report of July 12, 1919: "Drawing incline 60°—3x5 foot section driven to cut 7 ft. thick oil shale bed. Shale to be dropped through this raise to bulkhead loading station, loaded on mine cars and run a distance of 200 ft. to jig-back terminal on tramway.

Fig. 38—*Condensing pipes and boxes of plant of The Mount Logan Oil Shale and Refining Company, near De Beque, Colorado.* (*From* The Shale Review, *May,* 1920.)

Fig. 39—*The Mount Logan Oil Shale and Refining Company, showing Mount Logan in background. The cliff in foreground is not oil shale.* (*From* The Shale Review, 1919.)

"*Incline*—46° 30 and 85 ft. long, 4 ft. x 4 ft. [in sections] average 50 cubic yards—about 100 tons.

"*Tramway*—Mine to bin about center of tram. Re-load and tram to plant.

"*Sample Cut*—Above mine 30 ft. wide, 13 ft. long and 6 ft. high = 43.3 cu. yds. shale was reported 28 gallons per ton.

"*House Cave*—19.5 ft. long, 7 ft. high, 9 ft. wide = 45.5 cu. yds."

1920—Colorado Bureau of Mines report: "Simplex type retort completed; not producing."

1921—Colorado Bureau of Mines report: "Began work February 13, 1921, and intermittent until July 14, 1921; 10 ft. of tunnel [driven]; treated 35 tons shale; produced 52 barrels of oil; 1–30 ton car shale shipped [Dannville, Pennsylvania]."

1921—*The Shale Review*, April: "Mt. Logan running at different times for several months. A recent fire destroyed some of their first product and interrupted operations [15 barrels oil reported burned]."

1921—*The Shale Review,* May: "Mt. Logan not able to complete 80 barrel order due to snow and storms."

1921—*The Shale Review,* September: "Reported Mt. Logan shipped a carload of shale to Massachusetts School of Technology at Boston for tests to be made by the students."

1922—January 1922, a request to Henry Ford for assistance. The reply to this letter is shown in Figure 40.[105]

1922—Colorado Bureau of Mines Inspectors Report of February 17, 1923, for year 1922: "Inactive during year."

1923—Colorado Bureau of Mines Inspectors Report of July 17, 1924: "No work—not in operation."

1924—Colorado Bureau of Mines, February 17, 1925, report: "Not in operation."

The Mount Logan Oil Shale and Refining Company was a public stock company. The stock, although having a $0.01 par value, sold at prices of $0.25 per share, $0.75 per share, and $1.00 per share.[106] By December 1920, the corporation was having difficulty raising money.[107] The company could not sell stock fast enough and had to close down.[108] One of the officers, H. D. Locke, stayed on in De Beque continuing with assessment work in the form of road repair to maintain the company's mining claims.[109] He also unsuccess-

fully tried to interest others in financially backing the company. But no new operations were ever started at the plant and the corporation became defunct on October 25, 1926.[110]

The Oil Shale Mining Company

This company erected the first working retort in western Colorado and produced small amounts of shale oil.

Organized	:	October 2, 1916, State of Colorado
Capitalized	:	$250,000.00—250,000 shares par value $1.00
President	:	Harry Flynn
Vice-President	:	Unknown
Secretary-Treasurer	:	Charles E. Flynn
Property	:	960 acres
Location	:	Dry Fork, 20 miles northwest of De Beque
Plant	:	First retort erected in Colorado. This was a "Henderson" retort. Later a "Youngs" retort was tested
Mine	:	Shale obtained from outcrop. A tramway was constructed but probably never used
Production	:	30 barrels of shale oil

The Oil Shale Mining Company was incorporated under the laws of the State of Colorado on October 2, 1916.[111] All the incorporators and original officers of the corporation were from the towns of Palisade and Rifle, Colorado, in the vicinity of the oil shale fields.[112]

By the end of 1916, this company had built a bunkhouse and a cookhouse.[113] By the end of the following year, the company had moved the buildings to a new location (Fig 41), added a log cabin, moved machinery in for retorting, and built a lumber chute down to the retorts.[114] Martin Gavin of the U.S. Bureau of Mines [115] describes this operation as follows:

"In 1916, a small retort, said to be a modification of the Scotch Henderson, was erected near De Beque, Colorado. Except for minor details, this retort was all the modern Henderson is not. It was of cast iron with 1-inch walls, 15 feet high and tapering, 12-inches in diameter at the top and 20-inches at the bottom. A piece of 12-inch casing, 8-feet long, set vertically at the top, served as a hopper, and a one-toothed roller at the bottom,

Henry Ford
Dearborn, Mich.

Jan
27th
1922

Mount Logan Oil Shale M & R Co
De Beque
Colorado

Gentlemen: Attention Mr H D Locke, Secretary

            Your letter of recent date, addressed

to Mr Ford, has been handed the writer for reply.

            Mr Ford does not make investments of

any nature, and consequently would not be interest-

ed in the matter referred to in your letter.

            Thanking you, however, for submitting

the same for his consideration, I am

                Very truly yours

                V L SHEVLIN
                Asst Secretary to HENRY FORD

    VLS H

Fig. 40—Reply by Henry Ford to a request by The Mount Logan Oil Shale and Refining Company for assistance. (From Department of the Interior.)

Fig. 41—*View of the properties of The Oil Shale Mining Company on Dry Fork, near De Beque, Colorado. Note camp in foreground and site of Young and Henderson retorts.* (*From* The Shale Review, *December,* 1919.)

operated intermittently by hand, was intended as a discharge mechanism. The retort was set in a brick furnace, not at all like that used with the Henderson retort, and was heated by combustion of the gases produced in retorting, supplemented by raw shale burned in a fire box. A small exhaust pump drew vapors away from the retort. Provision was made for passing steam into the bottom of the retort.

"The retort was filled with rich massive shales, and heated. As is probably the case with many rich shales, when heated rapidly, this shale intumesced [swelled] and adhered to the walls of the retort, stopping operations. From the results of this one retort, the idea has risen that Scotch retorts can not be used for rich American shales. By referring to the description of the Henderson retort it is evident that the retort under discussion was a crude attempt to imitate it. The test was by no means fair, and should not be considered conclusive. One of the features of the Scotch retort is the fact that the shales are heated slowly, and the products removed rapidly by the use of excessive quantities of steam. As far as coking or adhering of the shales to the walls is concerned, experiments conducted by the Bureau of Mines indicate that these difficulties can be avoided with most shales if they are heated slowly and the products removed as they are formed. Later tests on the type of retort referred to above, somewhat modified, have given more favorable results, but even yet it is by no means more than a crude

attempt to imitate the modern Scotch retort."

The retort was a noncontinuous or batch-type retort with a capacity of around 6–10 tons of shale per day. "Material for a total of six Henderson retorts is on the ground."[116] The records do not indicate they were ever erected.

Early attempts to obtain shale for the retort were described in the *Railroad Red Book* of January 1921, as follows:

"The Oil Shale Mining Company several years ago installed a sheet-iron, open chute at its property at the head of Dry Fork but the arrangements proved absolutely unsatisfactory and was abandoned."

In 1919, a tramway was constructed (Fig 42) but apparently never used. This tramway was to connect the new mill site with the quarry after the failure of the open chute mentioned above.

This tramway was described and commented upon by an Inspector for the General Land Office[117] as follows:

". . . According to Harry Flynn this tramway was constructed in 1919. Also two buckets were constructed for use of the tramway, but we learned that they were never used and they were lying near the road some distance from the tramway.

"The tramway was so poorly constructed that it never could be used with safety, and so far as we learned, it was never used.

"We interviewed J. W. McBeth, at Palisade, Colorado on June 28, 1929 and learned that he was working for Flynn at the time this tramway was constructed, and had charge of the camp. He stated the following as to this tramway: [This statement has been abstracted to reduce its length.] 'Flynn had two spools of 1½ inch second-hand cables he bought from the Garfield [Coal] mine at Palisade after the mine had thrown it away. . . . McBeth told Flynn that it was only junk and he didn't believe the inspectors would allow him to put it up and Flynn said he had only paid a junk price for it. . . . They didn't put any of

the cable or tramway up while McBeth was there, but did it the next spring. . . . McBeth said he heard at De Beque that the inspector of mines came there and didn't let them use the tramway.' "A man named Axel V. Young made the buckets for the tramway—he filed a lien against the claims for labor, on June 10, 1925, which was later taken care of by L. D. Crandell."

When the author visited this site, the cable and towers were in place (Fig 42). There was no evidence of

Fig. 42—View from anchor point looking down the tramway of the Oil Shale Mining Company on Dry Forks. (1967 photograph by author.)

loading facilities or unloading facilities nor any other evidence to indicate the tramway ever had been used. Mr. Randall, a local rancher, reported he had worked in the area during the 1920s and that shale needed for the retorts had been transported on "stone boats", pulled by horses down the ridge below the cableway to a point above the retort. (Also reported by Inspector, General Land Office.)[118]

During 1919, the company experimented with a continuous type of retort invented by its superintendent, A. V. Young.[119] But later that year, the Young invention was abandoned by the company and it returned to use of the batch type "Henderson" retort.[120] During these years the company improved the road leading to the camp, removed some shale from the cliffs and occasionally ran its retort. C. L. Jones of the Mellon Institute[121] described both the Young retort and The Oil Shale Mining Company's Henderson retort as follows:

"This company first worked on the so-called 'Young Continuous' retort, which the writer saw. This retort seems to be made from a short piece of coal chute, covered with sheet iron, and provided with scrapers fastened to an endless chain operated by a hand crank. The shale is fed into the top of the chute, scraped through it by means of this crank, and drawn off from the bottom of the chute through a water seal. A wood fire is built under the apparatus.

"This company now offers shale oil for sale which is made in what is claimed to be a 'Henderson' retort. This retort, however, has little in common with the well known Henderson Scotch retort. It is a piece of oil well casing holding about 500 pounds of shale, direct heated by a wood or shale fire, and charged intermittently. The market is believed to be dull."

In 1920, the company intermittently shipped a few barrels or gallons of shale oil, but not much oil was produced.[122] During 1921, the total production of the plant was 30 barrels of shale oil.[123] At first the company planned to make profits by manufacturing inexpensive retorts.[124] However, a duplicate retort was tried elsewhere in the oil shale field and coked up so badly it was discarded.[125] This corporation then stressed a multitude of chemical products that could be made from shale oil, including sheep dip, wood preservers, flotation oil, leather preserver, water proofer, medicated soap, mechanics soap and other products.[126]

Events in the life of this company have been compiled chronologically and follow:

1916—First work done was by Harry Flynn, and J. W. Richards: built cookhouse and bunkhouse.

1917—Combined cookhouse and bunkhouse moved. Large log cabin constructed. Road constructed. Built plant site No. 1 with several retorts and other machinery. Open pit mining with lumber chute down to the retort. Retorts made sample runs.

1918—Took oil shale samples and tested them in the retorts. In fall of 1918 decided to move retort farther down canyon. Prepared new site.

1919—Rebuilt plant at plant site No. 2. Continued sampling and testing these in the retorts. Built a tramway.

1920—Most of the work was running samples through the retorts.

1921—Assessment work. Made considerable runs in the retorts testing out oil shales. This was the last year that any testing was done in the retorts. 20 tons of shale retorted, 30 barrels of oil produced.

1923 through 1929—Assessment work only.[127]

The Oil Shale Mining Company was a public stock company. About 62,000 shares of its stock were sold at prices between $0.50 and $1.00[128] and probably around $35,000 was raised.[129] After May 1922 there was no more sales of stock by this company.[130] Five thousand dollars ($5,000.00) was the largest amount that was borrowed at one time, and this was in 1925.[131] After stockholders ceased putting up money and new stock ceased to be sold, the company failed to keep up even the assessment work on the mining claims.[132] Formula, machinery, shale land and options were valued at about $24,400.00 in the annual report filed with the Secretary of the State of Colorado on July 13, 1926.[133]

The company's mining claims were subjected to legal attachments, and by 1926 it had lost its properties.[134] On October 12, 1931, the corporation became defunct.[135] Figure 43 shows the remains of the Henderson retort as seen by the author in 1967. A copy of the company prospectus (Fig. 44) is reproduced to provide additional information regarding the company.

Flynn failed to do assessment work and lost the claims in 1926 to L. D. Crandell, who had loaned considerable money to Flynn. Crandell gained title to the claims and attempted to do assessment work but was financially unable to do so. Most of the claims were in default.[136]

In the summer of 1929, the Shale Oil and By-Products Company of Chicago started work. They took possession of the cabins claiming that they had a lease from the present homesteaders for the land on which the cabins were located. As a result, a dispute arose between Flynn and the Chicago oil shale group. Flynn then posted notices on the cabins and on the tramway stating that it was the sole property of S. G. McMullen, who was a banker in Grand Junction, Colorado.[137]

The Shale Oil and By-Products Company did some road improvement but never constructed a retort or produced any oil.

Thus, total production appears to have been from 30 to possibly 35 barrels of oil, all of which seems to have been produced in 1921 and earlier years. The company was under-financed and had little technical knowledge of the problems it attempted to solve.

Fig. 43—Remains of the Henderson retort of The Oil Shale Mining Company on Dry Forks. (1967 photograph by author.)

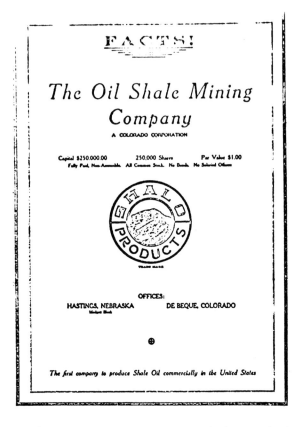

FACTS!

The Oil Shale Mining Company

A COLORADO CORPORATION

Capital $250,000.00   250,000 Shares   Par Value $1.00

Fully Paid, Non-Assessable. All Common Stock. No Bonds. No Salaried Officers

OFFICES:

HASTINGS, NEBRASKA   DE BEQUE, COLORADO

⊕

The first company to produce Shale Oil commercially in the United States

The richness of our shales. Picked samples have run as high as 110 gallons of oil to the ton of shale. Our general average has been fifty to sixty-five gallons to the ton.

Some Essentials

When investigating a proposition it is needful to a certain whether or not the company has the essentials to succeed. Have they an abundance of raw materials? Have they the means of turning, economically, these raw materials into a commercial product? Have they fuel, water, timbers, and everything needful for the success of the project? Have they got the building sites? Are they located near to transportation? Are their products in demand? Does the manufacture of these products require extensive equipment and skilled labor? Is the company efficiently officered and managed?

We Have Every Essential

Our company has every qualification noted above. Our raw materials, high grade shale, may be seen and measured with a rule. We have a successful process proven by four years of satisfactory operation. Ample fuel, water and timbers. Our building sites are ideal. So located that we may grow and grow indefinitely and still be able to dump the spent shale (waste) in the gulch below. Our camp and mine is located twenty miles from the Denver & Rio Grande Railroad and the town of DeBeque, Colorado. We have a good mountain road from our camp to the railroad. As the haul is all down grade enormous loads may be transported by truck and trailer. In time a pipe line will convey our products by gravity from our plant to storage tanks at the railroad station. A ready market for all our products is assured and at a profitable prices. No expensive equipment will be required to manufacture all our "Shalo Products." Only a nominal number of skilled employes will be required, manual labor will be largely used, as well as labor saving machines.

Our Officers and Directors

Are all men of business ability and experience. We venture the assertion that no company in any line of endeavor can show better management or more judicious economy in the expenditure of the stockholders money. The more you investigate The Oil Shale Mining Company the better you are going to like it and the better we will like it.

The Value of Our 960 Acres Shale Land

That the reader may get some idea of shale land values we quote from the Colorado School of Mines Quarterly for October 1919 as follows:

"When we consider the enormous oil content of these lands and that engineers can sample, measure and prove up the tonnage and estimate to a certainty that each acre of these choice lands contains fifty thousand barrels and upwards of oil that can be recovered certainly and cheaply, and that each ton of oil shale is of much more value and profit than a ton of coal, and as coal in place in the ground sells at from three to ten cents a ton, then oil shales are certainly worth as much or more per ton, and at a valuation of but one cent per ton or one cent per barrel for oil, they are worth $500 an acre, while a fair valuation of but ten cents a barrel for "oil in place" would make the land worth $5,000 an acre." We are not talking petroleum—one gallon of shale oil we consider of more value than five gallons of well oil—the above quotation is given only to show you that we have ample oil for making our "Shalo Products" in great commercial quantities for hundreds of years.

Our Shalo Products

Some of the numerous products we manufacture under our trade mark name "Shalo Products," are noted on the following page. This trade mark will cover all our products from a cake of soap to a tank car of dip.

This is an oil shale mining proposition of a speculative nature and the profits to be derived therefrom will wholly depend upon the company and mineral values the company may be able to extract from shale oil. No specific profits are guaranteed. Stock salesmen receive fifteen per cent commission. Authorized and issued by virtue of Permit No. 288 granted by the Nebraska Bureau of Securities under date of September 13th, 1920. The Bureau does not recommend nor disparage investment in any securities favored by it.

History

The Oil Shale Mining Company is a Colorado corporation. Organized in October 1916. We made our first run in the presence of a number of interested scientific men and spectators, on July 1st, 1917. Photographs of the original retort were made at the time of this run and have been published in The National Geographic Magazine, Munsey's, The Railroad Red Book, Motor Age, The Shale Review, and many statistical bulletins, daily news papers and magazines throughout the country. This run and the photograph of the same is of considerable scientific importance by reason of the fact that this was The First Retort Erected In The United States That Successfully Produced Commercial Quantities Of Shale Oil.

Our Property and Location

The Oil Shale Mining Company own 960 acres of exceptionally rich shale lands. These lands are located on Dry Fork, in Garfield County, Colorado, twenty miles Northwest of DeBeque. We have a good mountain road from our mine and plant to the D. & R. G. Railroad station. We have an abundance of cold mountain spring water so situated that it may be easily and cheaply piped, under pressure, to our plant for compounding manufacturing and domestic purposes as well as fire protection.

Timbers Fuel and Lumber in Abundance

In selecting this land for our company we not only had in mind the fact that we must have practically an unlimited amount of workable high-grade shales—accessible and near to transportation—we must also have ample supplies of fuel, timbers and lumber available for manufacturing purposes. These we have in great abundance.

Our Equipment

We have good buildings at our mine and camp for housing and feeding our men. We have an option on a modern brick building, in the heart of Hastings' wholesale district. We shall establish in this building our laboratory, factory and executive offices, each equipped with every needful device. In this plant we will build on a large scale and economically all our "Shalo Products."

We have on the good eight Henderson (Scottish type) retorts, two of which are now installed and producing oil. The other six retorts we expect to install soon. With this equipment installed and operating twenty-four hours a day we will be able to produce sufficient shale oil for the manufacture of our various "Shalo Products" on a large commercial scale. This plant is so arranged that units may be added as our requirements demand and at a moderate cost.

A 2000 Foot Tramway

Is being erected for the purpose of transporting the shale from the shale beds to our retorts. This tramway has a capacity of 150 tons per day. The aerial tramway is an ideal method of transporting such commodities as shale. It requires no power other than the two buckets—the full bucket or car serving as the motive power to return to the shale beds the empty bucket. These cars or "tram-buckets" are absolutely controlled by one man at the top operating two levers. The stability of this tramway must be seen to be appreciated.

Retorting Process Simple

The process of extracting the crude oil from shale is the age old method of destructive distillation. The shale is broken to suitable size placed in an iron retort, heat is applied to the retort the gases are driven off and condensed forming the crude petroleum. Many good processes have been ruined by complicating them. Our process is the simplest form and has passed the experimental stage. In retorting shale we have a quantity of fixed gases that have great heat value. One ton of our shale will produce during the process of retorting about 3000 cubic feet of gas. The equivalent of about 300 pounds of coal in heat value. We will utilize this gas by piping it back under the retort for heating purposes. Once the retorts are heated this fixed gas will go a long way towards retorting the shale. A shale plant with 400 tons daily capacity would produce in gas the equivalent of about thirty-eight tons of coal.

Shalo Animal Dip and Disinfectant

An animal dip and disinfectant for the treatment of Lice, Mites, Skin Diseases, Wounds, Mange, Scab in live stock and poultry. Non-caustic yet powerful and certain in its action. We supply patrons with instructions for making concrete hog wallows and dipping vats. The sale of dip in the U. S. is large—our prices will be under legitimate competition. Our profits large. Shalo dip—a business by itself.

Shalo Wood Preserver

Sixty per cent of our original forests have disappeared. We use four times as much timber as is grown each year. We are nearing a timber famine. Wood preservation is our imperative need. Our preserver has great penetrating powers. It keeps out moisture. It destroys vermin. It preserves wood. The wood preserving field is as large as the nation. Every Railroad company, every telephone and telegraph company, every farmer, every home builder, every person who uses wood is a possible patron of ours for wood preserver. Applied in every way, hot or cold, open tank, brush, spraying, dipping treatment all are effectual with our Shalo Wood Preserver. Two or three companies with millions of capital depend upon this alone for revenue and pay satisfactory dividends. They get their raw materials from abroad or in the open market—we take ours out of shale rock—draw your own conclusions.

Shalo Flotation Oil

A tremendous field is just opening at this time for the sale of our "Shalo Flotation Oil." Mr. James M. McClave, a man skilled in flotation oils says in part "After over 100 varieties of oil had been experimented with, and as a last resort, the shale oil was tested on the ore with surprising results. After complete failure with pine oil, and various combinations, the shale oil produced clean concentrates with a high recovery. "Shalo Flotation Oil" is a success and shale oil sold as such will bring about eight times as much as crude oil thus giving the reader some idea of this as a profitable field.

Shalo Leather Preserver and Water Proofer

Another wonderful "Shalo Product." It is impossible to describe its action. Must be used to be fully appreciated. Makes hard and lifeless leather soft and pliable. Waterproofs, preserves and softens all leather and lengthens its life. Easily applied not "greasy". Made from Shalo Oil of course. Other companies have built a profitable business on leather dressings much inferior to this. An ideal dressing for bolting, harness, shoes, gloves, and all leather.

Shalo Medicated Scalp and Skin Soap

A recent arrival in the "Shalo Family." Just the best scalp treatment and shampoo ever devised. The ladies are delighted with "Shalo Shampoo." A soap that's different. A healing, soothing, cleansing, delightful toilet soap. Nothing like it on the market. It has no competitor. Sale will be large. The profits good.

Shalo Mechanics Soap

A soap to cleanse the grimy hands of workers in grease and dirt. Leaves the hands soft and free from chaps. Soothing and healing. Something new in abrasive soaps. We predict a large and profitable sale.

Many Other Shalo Products

Our chemists are constantly doing research work for the exclusive benefit of The Oil Shale Mining Company. Below we merely mention the names of a few other "Shalo Products" for man and beast. "Shalo Skidoo" keeps flies away—they do "skidoo." "Shalo Lice Killer" the poultry keepers friend. "Shalo Ointment" an analgesic, antiseptic healing salve for wire cuts, galls, chafes, open wounds, for man or beast. It is wonderful. Once used no home will be without it. "Shalo Scalp and Dandruff Treatment." A new hair treatment. Will grow hair if the hair roots are not dead. The manufacture of these last named "Shalo Specialties" would alone be enough for a large company. We give our stockholders the benefit of all our efforts.

THE OIL SHALE MINING COMPANY

HASTINGS, NEBRASKA   DE BEQUE, COLORADO

Fig. 44—Prospectus, The Oil Shale Mining Company. (*From Department of the Interior.*)

The Searchlight Oil Shale
& Refining Company

Organized	:	Originally incorporated as Searchlight Oil & Mining Company, March 4, 1918, State of Colorado. On August 20, 1920, it changed its name to Searchlight Oil Shale and Refining Company
Capitalized	:	$250,000 par value $0.10 per share
President	:	A. G. Dominey
Vice-President	:	Robert J. Verner
Treasurer and General Manager	:	Robert E. McGee
Property	:	1,120 acres
Location	:	On Clear Creek, 18 miles north of De Beque
Plant	:	None. One proposed in Denver but never built
Mine	:	None
Production	:	None

Originally, the corporation dealt mainly in well petroleum.[138] By 1920 its emphasis changed to oil shale.

The Shale Review of December 1920 described the proposed operations of this company as follows:

"The Searchlight Oil Shale & Refining Company, of which Robert E. McGee is treasurer and general manager, will erect a shale treating retort and refinery of large capacity on property which has recently been leased for a period of years. The location is 1835 South Bannock Street, Denver, across the railroad from Overland Park. The grounds have an area of five acres. . . .

"The operation of this corporation will be along entirely different lines from those planned by most shale companies. It is proposed to ship crude shale from De Beque to Denver, specializing in certain by-products which bring high prices. It is also proposed to make bricks from spent shale. It is believed that labor conditions and the ready market for the output will more than offset the cost of shipping shale from the point at which it is mined. Experiments have been under way for several months in the company's laboratory in connection with the recovery of the analine fraction of shale oil for the purpose of manufacturing dyes. The results obtained in these tests have been remarkable and have been sufficiently successful to satisfy the management that fast dyes can be made from this oil and sold in the market at a very fancy profit. Experimenting has also been under way in connection with paints and house roofing material, as well as briquettes and coke. The recovery of oil by the Searchlight Company will be conducted in somewhat the same manner as other methods of treating shale, but the oil products will be only an incident of the business. The retort for which plans are already drawn, will have a capacity of 250 tons of shale daily."

The March 1921 issue of *The Shale Review* reported:

"Pittsburgh Brewery converted to Shale Retort—Since the advent of prohibition brewing plants throughout the United States have been seeking some form of manufacturing enterprise with which to utilize their idle plants. A field of usefulness for these buildings and machinery is offered in the shale industry. Robert E. McGee, of Denver, manager of the Searchlight Oil Shale Company, is now in Pittsburgh negotiating with the Pittsburgh Brewing Company for the conversion of a portion of their plant into a factory for the manufacture of analine dyes by the distillation of shale oil. Demonstrations have been made at the Mellon Institute with great success. If negotiations, now under way, are completed, it is planned to ship the crude shale from the west to the point of treatment. It is believed that the low freight rate on shale will justify its handling at the point of distribution as a manufactured material, if shipped to eastern markets, would require a much higher rate of freight. It is stated that a retort will be constructed which can handle at least 100 tons of shale daily and will be enlarged as business conditions justify. Under the system being worked out by Mr. McGee there is practically no refuse as all the volume of the shale is utilized."

In 1922, Robert E. McGee was reported to have been in Pittsburgh for the past year and was expected to return in a short time [to Colorado]. McGee stated he was ". . . installing a Stalmann retort and a Wells Refinery near Chillicothe, Ohio", and the ". . . construction work on the McGee plants is being formed at Pittsburgh and the equipment will be shipped from there to the point of operation."[139]

Fig. 45—Property of The Searchlight Oil Shale & Refining Company on Clear Creek, Garfield County, Colorado. (From The Shale Review, *July–August,* 1922.)

The Colorado Bureau of Mines Inspectors report for January 6, 1923, reported for The Searchlight Company, "assessment work with a few men during 1922." Figure 45 shows the property area.

There is no evidence that this corporation ever erected a retort anywhere, despite contrary claims. There are no records of oil ever having been produced.

A letter to the U.S. Land Office in Glenwood Springs, Colorado, dated December 3, 1926, read as follows:

> ". . . Mr. C. W. Darrow is attorney for the owners of these claims. Mr. Robert E. McGee and The Searchlight Oil Shale & Refining Company are the owners. Robert E. McGee formerly resided at the Kenmark Hotel in Denver but our information is that he was forced to take a hasty leave from Colorado. . . . We are unable to give his present address. Certain people in Denver are anxious to learn where it is."

The Searchlight Oil Shale & Refining Company became defunct and inactive in 1926.

Union Oil Co. of California, Inc.

The Union Oil Company was the most active of the major oil companies during the 1920s but its interest was only in obtaining oil shale lands. Union was the first large oil company to buy oil shale land when it purchased unpatented claims in 1921, subject to their being patented.[140] A 1920 report[141] stated:

> "On September 6, W. C. Orcult, engineer for the Union Oil Company of California, with four associates, was examining certain Parachute (Creek) properties."

V. C. Alderson reported in 1921 that the Union Oil Company was carrying 15,000 acres of land to patent.[142] Winchester[143] described Union's activities in 1922 as follows:

> ". . . By July 1, 1922 (Union) had made applications for practically all of its 17,000 acres of oil-shale placer claims near the forks of Parachute Creek, north of Grand Valley. The company has acquired a considerable area of ranch land adjacent to its oil shale property, to be used as a camp, reduction and waste dump sites in connection with the development of the oil shale. It also owns 200 acres near Grand Valley which is to be used for reduction and refinery operations. The company's research work during 1921 included the careful mapping of the oil shale outcrops on the property, the careful and complete sectioning and sampling of the Green River formation (2,300 ft.

thick), the making of about 6000 laboratory tests on 900 samples of oil shale, and the shipment of several large samples of the shale to the company's laboratories in California, where the shale is being used in extensive research operations. The company's field camp 12 miles north of Grand Valley includes three well constructed buildings, one of which is used as a field laboratory."

The *Railroad Red Book* of January 1922 described the sampling operation by Winchester as follows:

> ". . . a complete channel cut has been made, 2,300 feet in height, virtually from grass roots to the Wasatch formation, the weathered surface removed, and then each stratum sampled in the field and checked in the laboratory."

The Union Oil Company has continued its interest in oil shale land and has patented most or all of its holdings in Colorado. This continuing interest ultimately resulted in the opening of an oil shale mine and the construction of retorting facilities on Union's Parachute Creek holdings in 1957. The operation of this plant is described under "1940–1969" later in this book, and pictures of the operation are presented.

Ventura–Colorado Oil Company

The holdings described were the basis of the present oil shale holdings of the Texas Company.

Organized	:	May 17, 1922 State of Maine
Capitalized	:	$300,000 or 3,000 shares of $100 each. (All owned by Oak Ridge Oil Company. The latter's capital stock, in turn, is owned by California Petroleum Corporation (California)
President	:	Jacques Vinmont
Vice-President	:	F. C. Van Deinse
Secretary	:	D. E. O'Brien
Treasurer	:	W. D. Stewart
Property	:	9,406.73 acres of patented oil shale lands, plus some 1000 acres of ranch lands
Location	:	Garfield County, Colorado
Plant	:	Camp for exploration crews only
Mine	:	None
Production	:	None

The Ventura–Colorado Oil Company was organized for the purpose of acquiring title to certain oil shale deposits and ranch lands in Garfield County, Colo.

The properties consist of: The Burns Ranch, 572 acres; the Phares Ranch, 200 acres; and the Boyd Ranch, 280 acres; together with all improvements thereon and certain ditch and water rights appurtenant to said lands; and 9,726.50 acres, more or less, of oil shale deposits. United States patents [are held] covering 9,405.73 acres of the oil shale deposits.

Ventura–Colorado Oil Company on February 29, 1928, had invested a total of $358,585.99 in the foregoing properties.

In 1927 the properties were assessed by the County of Garfield on the basis of a value of $49,325.00 for the three ranches, $11,695 for the headquarters camp, and $4.00 per acre for the deposit claims.

The properties were under lease for agricultural and grazing purposes.[144]

During 1921, the corporation employed a contractor to diamond drill three exploration holes extracting 1½-inch core for analysis.[145] Also in 1921 trails and roads were constructed to the top of the oil shale escarpments. [This work was for assessment work on claims.]

In January 1922 it was reported:[146]

"The Ventura Consolidated Oil Fields Company of California, under the guidance of W. S. Skinner, has established a camp for 25 men and has diamond drilled its property by means of three boreholes, starting at different elevations so as to get a core representing 1600 feet. By this means the thickness of each stratum and its oil yield can be determined."

The following was published in January 1923:[147]

"The Ventura Consolidated Oilfields Company has made applications for Government patent on 5000 acres in addition to the acreage applied for in 1921. The holdings of this company on Brush Creek amount to 10,000 acres, all of which has been fenced at a cost of $7,000. In addition to the oil shale land acquired the company has purchased ranch and grazing land so as to have control of a large tract. To test the deposits accurately diamond drill holes have been put down so that the company has secured exact and detailed information of the thickness of each stratum of oil shale, its yield, and its geographic extent."

All holdings of this company were taken over by the Texas Company in 1928 by purchase of the parent corporation.

Washington Shale Oil & Products Company

Organized	:	August 11, 1920 State of Washington
Capitalized	:	$300,000—300,000 shares par value $1.00 per share
President	:	C. Orville White
Vice-President	:	Henry J. Gorin
Secretary	:	C. H. Jelsett
Property	:	200 acres shale land, 10 acres plant site
Location	:	Conn Creek, about 14 miles north of De Beque
Plant	:	First erected a Ginet retort, later erected a "White" retort
Mine	:	Tunnel 80 feet into cliff
Production	:	Some oil in 1927

The Washington Shale Oil & Products Company started building its plant in October 1921.[148] The Inspectors report for January 7, 1923,[149] reported the following:

"Washington Shale Company, Agent Mr. White, 722 Symes Bldg., Denver, Colo.

"Have new Ginet retort also several carloads of machinery supplies, etc., on the ground. . . . 12 men on assessment and other work during summer of 1922."

The literature did not contain information of any further activity until July 1925 when it was reported that this plant would be in operation before the first of the year [1926], and this would be the first plant to operate continuously in this State [Colorado].[150] In December it was reported:[151]

". . . The Washington Shale Oil & Products Company . . . is now in the course of construction on that company's large holdings on Conn Creek. . . .

"The 50-ton Ginet retort consists of a horizontal cylinder 3 feet in diameter and 20 feet long, within which is a series of scoops that revolve on a center shaft, lifting and showering the shale, and so arranged in series that the crushed shale particles are kept moving gradually through the length of the retort until the residue is taken out at the opposite end in the form of a perfectly dry powder.

"... The furnace is of special design, and is equipped with both gas and oil burners, the oil burners being used until sufficient gas is accumulated in the gas meter to furnish fuel for the gas burners.

"The oil vapors, or gas thrown off as the shale passes through the retort, rise to the top of the retort and are drawn off through six vertical tubes that connect with a manifold running parallel with the retort. From the manifold the gas is piped into large storage tanks. Here the ammonia water is drained off, and the gas is moved on to condensers, here the gas vapors are converted into crude oil which is conveyed by pipe to crude oil tanks, which are of 2,000 barrel capacity. The crude oil is then conveyed to a fractionating still where gasoline and other by-products are taken off."

Fig. 46—View of plant site, with tramway, of the Washington Shale Oil & Products Company, Conn Creek, north of De Beque, Colorado. (1967 photograph by author.)

A June 20, 1926, Inspectors report stated:[152]

"... Mine is opened by a tunnel about 4 x 6, 80 feet long. No work is being done in this tunnel at the present time. This company is completing an oil shale plant which is known as the Ginet Retort. A surface tram 2100 feet in length on a thirty-eight degree pitch is under construction. An electric-geared double drum hoist with safety devices attached to the car will be placed on this track. This car is built low in front and high on the rear wheels in order to ride level on this thirty-eight degree pitch. It will be used for handling men and supplies. Shale will be dropped down through a steel lined chute to a 200-ton capacity storage bin. This shale will be crushed in the escarpment or the portal of the tunnel before being dropped into the above mentioned chute. The Ginet Retort has just been completed and has a capacity of 100 tons daily.

"Fourteen buildings of frame construction are on this property. The company will generate its own electric power with a 150 horse power gas engine. They expect to run this engine on their own gas in the near future. An 80-foot concrete line shaft has been sunk to this distance for water purposes."

This Ginet retort was reported to be near operation in November 1926[153] and again in February 1927.[154] First operation was noted in November 1927 when it was reported:

"Work at present consists of installing a new White continuous retort. This retort is 100 feet long and consists of 20, 5 foot sections on 45 degree angles, and is made of fire brick with the inside size of 4 x 24 inches. The angles in this retort are put in with the idea of turning over the shale on its movement through the retorting process; also to pick it up after it passes over these angles. This retort is built on steel trestles varying in height, up the face of the mountain.

"This company is also installing new Ideal crushers for the purpose of grinding their shale as fine as possible in order that it may cook or roast within sixty seconds. Their present equipment consists of two large Gyratory crushers.

"On a recent run [using the Ginet retort] the following results were obtained from their shale on straight distillation: Gas content, 50%; kerosene, 12%; light oils, 15% and lubricating oils, 37%.

"Mr. White intends to have the new continuous retort in operation within the next thirty days. A great deal of experimental work has been done with this retort on a small scale in the companies' laboratories. Mr. White claims wonderful results for the White retort. Very little shale has been mined for some time past and none will be mined until the retort is running up to capacity. . . . Six men are employed."[155]

The corporation was still in the process of construction in 1929, and commercial operations had not been started.[156] Some oil was produced in 1927, but the amount was small.[157] Figure 46 shows the plant site as it appeared in 1967.

Total cost of the plant was about $85,000 with a total of $145,611.58 in assets loss, assignment of contracts, land and advances.[158]

On July 1, 1935, the Washington Shale Oil & Products Company was automatically dissolved for failure over a 5 year period to pay its license in the State of Washington.[159]

MONTANA ACTIVITIES

Dillon Oil Company [Later, *Smallhorn Oil Shale and Refining Company*]

This Montana oil shale operation, like the one in New Brunswick, was active during the same time as those in Utah, Nevada, Wyoming and Colorado, and is included because it was one of the few that actually constructed a retort on the property (Fig 47).

Dean E. Winchester[160] of the U.S. Geological Survey described the oil shale occurrences of the Montana area as follows:

"In West-central Montana oil shale occurs in formations of Tertiary, Permian, Pennsylvania, and Devonian age. Samples show that most of the shale beds, which are not very persistent, are very low-grade oil shales and only of scientific interest. In the area around Dillon and Dell, however, Phosphoria formation (Permian) contains 50 to 75 feet of phosphatic black shales, of which a few beds will yield 20 to 30 gallons of oil to the ton. A distillation retort installed at this location is said to have a capacity of 50 tons of shale per day. In the Western part of this area there is a belt of Tertiary oil shales about 28 miles long. Some of these shales, which occur in beds as much as 5 feet thick, will yield about 24 gallons of oil to the ton."

Victor C. Alderson, in 1920,[161] commented as follows:

Fig. 47—Galloupe shale retort of the Dillon Oil Company, Dillon, Montana. (From The Shale Review, *August, 1920.)*

"The oil shales of Montana, near Dillon, offer a new problem to the experimenter. They are peculiar in that they contain phosphoric acid and the beds are called phosphoric oil shale. . . . Richest shale beds are only three feet, does not exceed 30 gallons to the ton. The phosphate beds also are thin and contain but a small amount of phosphorus pentoxide."

In September 1920 the *National Petroleum News* published the following by H. L. Wood:

"Smallhorn Oil Shale Refining Company, Dillon, Montana. A Galloupe retort located twelve miles southeast of Dillon and six miles east of the Oregon Shortline Railroad. Promoted three years ago (1917) as the Dillon Oil Company, a reorganization was perfected some time ago, local people furnishing the capital, the company is now ready to add more retorts and begin commercial operation early next year with a 50-ton capacity, after an experimental investment of about $40,000, some of which was wasted. Plant is conveniently located between two hills of solid shale, with a good road to town, the ore coming from a horizontal excavation in the hill at a level to gravity the shale to the crusher and retort, the mine having been opened more than twenty years ago by persons who had discovered the shale carried oil while prospecting for coal. The shaft was cut to depth of 75 feet in solid massive shale that so far shows 17 gallons per ton. The Anaconda Copper Company is testing the crude oil, and if found satisfactory will take the entire output at $10 a barrel. The company is capitalized at $300,000."

The oil shale retort used during the 1920 efforts of the Smallhorn Oil and Refining Company was described by Hamor[162] as follows:

"The retort (a Galloupe) which is made of cast iron and is about 20 feet high, consists of two main parts, viz, an outer stationary shell, and an inner core constructed to revolve and carry the oil shale down through the retort. The outer shell is cast in segments 1 foot high having on their inner sides a series of staggered shelves projecting about 4 inches into the center. The inner core consists of a segmented, hollow cylinder with staggered fins projecting about 4 inches on the outside. When the retort is in operation, the core is suspended on ball bearings and revolved so that the finely crushed shale, which is fed continuously at the top, is scraped from each shelf to the one below by the fins of the core."

The reference to the Anaconda Copper Company's interest in shale oil is one of many references in the literature of the day that shale oil would find wide usage as flotation agents in beneficiation mills, such as those of Anaconda, for the recovery of mineral products. The Smallhorn plant produced some 15 barrels of oil by the mid-1920s, and further references to this operation were not found in the literature.

NEVADA ACTIVITIES

Figure 48 is a map of the Elko, Nevada, area showing the location of the Catlin Shale Products Company's plant and the Southern Pacific Railroad Company's plant.

Catlin Shale Products Company

The Catlin Shale operation at Elko, Nevada, represented the largest, best technically oriented and best financed effort to develop the western oil shales during the 1917-1930 period. Catlin's production of shale oil probably was in excess of 12,000 barrels. No western oil shale plant exceeded this total production until the Union Oil Company operation of 1957-58, on Parachute Creek, Colorado.

Catlin's operation was self-financed, with no public sales of stock. Visitors to the operation were not encouraged and publicity concerning its activities was not promoted. Descriptions of plant design and problems of operation were seldom released or discussed in public. The material presented here has been abstracted from information compiled by Mr. Vern Whitham,

Attorney, the Department of Interior Solicitor's Office, Denver, Colorado.[163]

The story of the Catlin Shale Products Company would require a separate volume to do it justice. The summation made here can only cover the highlights of the events that occurred.

According to the records, it can be said that the history of this operation covers a period of years starting in 1875 and ending in 1930. The start was noted by R. M. Catlin, Sr.[164] as follows:

"In June, 1875, I noted the presence of paraffin shale beds exposed by the C.P.R.R. Co. in their explorations of the lignite seams on the Humbolt River at Elko, Nevada. . . . My first contract to purchase shale land at Elko, Nevada was made in 1890 with the C.P.R.R. Co. who, as early as 1869, had spent considerable money in prospecting the lignite seams that occur throughout the Elko formation. . . . On November 24, 1890 from 100 lbs. of surface shale distilled in a quicksilver retort I obtained 22 lbs. of crude oil and 68 lbs. of spent shale or 53⅓ gallons of crude oil per ton."

Thus, as described in his own handwriting, began the experiments by Robert M. Catlin, which intermittently were to span one-half a century.

Robert Mayo Catlin was born on June 8, 1853, in Burlington, Vermont. At 22, after having graduated two years earlier from the University of Vermont, Catlin hired out as a mining engineer in Tuscarora, Nevada, a roaring mining community.[165]

Catlin subsequently purchased additional oil shale property from the Central Pacific Railroad in 1890[166], noting at the time:

"I continued experimenting and studying the matter until called to Johannesberg in 1895 where I was professionally engaged on other matters so that nothing further was done until after my return to this country."[167]

Catlin returned to the United States in 1906 to become employed at Franklin, New Jersey, with the New Jersey Zinc Company, but he did not resume oil shale experiments until 1912.[168] During 1915-1916, Catlin obtained still more land[169] and started development and research work.[170] By January 1916, an inclined shaft of 100 feet had been sunk, a laboratory built, and sampling, prospecting and research done.

On October 30, 1916, Catlin reported:[171]

"I have erected a 20-ton retort on my property at Elko, as situated in my lease, but do not expect to produce much this season, as the frost will cut off my water supply."

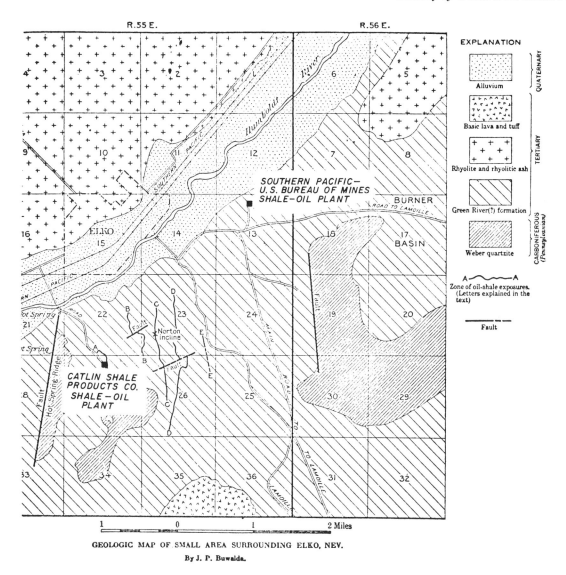

Fig. 48—Location of oil shale plants near Elko, Nevada. (From U.S. Geological Survey Bulletin 729.)

This retort was described by J. B. Mull[172] as follows: "This twenty-ton retort is the one described by Dean E. Winchester . . . as 'the first large-scale retort at Elko, consisting of four inclined tubes through which the shale was driven by auger-like screws, one in each tube. The tubes were heated from without and the oil vapors were drawn off at the lower end of the retort.' A considerable volume of oil was produced on this retort but as its operation was not entirely satisfactory, it was later dismantled."

Prior to the assembly of his second large-scale retort, Catlin formed a company. It was incorporated

in Delaware on November 26, 1917, bearing the name "Catlin Shale Products Company". Upon organization, Catlin received 1,840 shares of the stock valued at about $138.00 a share in exchange for his patents and oil shale land interests. Apparently 951 shares were sold for cash at about $138.00 each. This would have grossed the company some $131,000.[173] Formal transfer of the property was effected on March 11, 1918.[174]

Operator reports to the Inspector of Mines, State of Nevada, filed by the company for 1918 listed "Capital Stock—3000 shares, at no par value". The May 25, 1920, report showed "5000 shares—no par value".

The June 13, 1923, report showed 7500 shares and the May 23, 1925, report showed 12,500 shares. The May 21, 1928, report showed "No par value—7876 issued" [shares].

According to Winchester,[175] Catlin began assembly of his second large-scale retort in 1918, "even before the first plant had been given a thorough test. . . ."

Frank Wadleigh[176] (*Railroad Red Book*) reported that Catlin's second large-scale retort, a circular-cylindrical model, was "about 90 percent completed at the present time [Wadleigh visited Catlin in March 1919] and ought to be running within thirty- or forty-five days at the outside." He described the retort as eight circular retorts "surrounding a big cylindrical tank", indicating the arrangement with a diagram showing eight smaller circles surrounding a larger, central circle.

> "Each of the eight retorts is sixteen feet long by four feet in diameter. The big central tank is cylindrical and about eighteen or twenty feet in diameter, . . . There is a central core running through each of the eight retorts. . . . Heat is applied on the outside of the retorts and through the central core. This is so that there may be a uniformity in heat. The retorts and the central cylinder are insulated with 'diatomaceous earth', a white substance found near Carlin in Nevada and which is not phased by 1600 degrees of heat. The gases come off at the top at about 850 degrees and pass through one or more scrubbers. There is a big blower adjoining the scrubbers."

J. B. Mull[177] added:

> ". . . I believe that the central, large vessel was a gas producer for recovering heat for retorting by combustion of the fixed carbon remaining in the retorted shale."

W. L. Sheeler,[178] Superintendent, Catlin Shale Products Company, described the mining in 1920 as follows:

> "Elko Shales, Geologic period: Middle Miocene; strike: N.E. to S.W. dip: E22 degrees to 25 degrees, present mining on seam; average thickness five feet; inclined shaft on dip of vein, 22 degrees to 25 degrees; depth of shaft, 650 feet; electric hoisting; levels every 50 feet, north and south of the main incline, afford excellent ventilation; little timber used in mine; hanging wall stands well due to hard rib of lean shale above main seam; foot wall composed principally of clay decomposed rhyolite; shale mined with electric auger drills; no drill columns used, two men to

a drill; average number holes drilled in headings: forty six-foot depth per eight hour shift; seven holes to five by seven face; shale at present hand mucked to cars; cars trammed to pockets on different levels and from pockets discharged through chutes to slope cars; on bottom level cars run directly from incline slope onto level; mine stoped on south and along end line, to find out how ground acts when longwall retreating is started; in mucking, present plan is to install slusher operated by electric slusher hoists, and scrape directly into cars; mine free from dust as augers bore a coarse shale shaving; no gas in mine [methane]; shale shot from heading faces with 25 percent and 40 percent dynamite; mine at present making 25 gallons of water per minute; with exception of trial stope, all work done is to block out shale body; present output 100 tons of shale per 16 hours; mining as planned, using retreating longwall, cost per ton shale delivered to crusher is $1.00 or less."

Reports filed by the company with the Nevada Inspector of Mines showed the average amount of shale mined per month to be 3000 tons.[179] The report of June 13, 1923, noted ventilation raises to the surface north and south of the inclined shaft. No unusual conditions were ever noted in these reports and mine conditions were reported as good throughout the project.[180]

According to Wadleigh's notes, W. L. Sheeler (Catlin's superintendent) expressed to him the intent that they would first attempt to produce crude oil and then paraffin. Then they intended to recover gasoline and lubricating oils from the crude oil. This is a change from earlier indications of a desire to rely upon by-product output. In addition, Wadleigh[181] related in his memorandums:

> "They expect to put in a refinery at a point perhaps 150 feet from their retorts, the stills for which are at the station in Elko and will shortly be removed to the site of their operations. They have in place nine big oil tanks to receive their crude. One of these tanks contains about a thousand gallons, distilled by means of their demonstration plant last summer. They do not intend to go after the ammonium sulphate."

Wadleigh's last statement meant that Catlin had abandoned any hope, if he ever had such hope, of depending upon the product that had sustained the Scottish oil shale industry over the years.

On December 2, 1919, Sheeler advised Alderson that they were expecting the "Refrigerating plant, consisting of oil stills, agitator, and complete wax plant."[182]

The record is quite fragmentary regarding the operations of this second retort. There were both success and problems, as indicated by a July 1919 report:

"We made one run with the new plant producing five thousand gallons of oil. At present, we have stopt (sic) to make some changes which we think will be beneficial and will gain from the knowledge of the workings of the plant on our trial run. We hope to start up again in the near future and eliminate previous faults."

An August 6, 1919, letter from Catlin[183] to Wadleigh is quoted in its entirety because it reflects Catlin's aims and feelings regarding oil shale development:

"Re yours of July 29th just received. In regard to my process I may say that I have been trying out a number of devices and combinations and am uncertain just which you refer to as my process. The treatment depends on the original character of the shale and the products sought. I understand that you seek 'a process that will produce oil and its various by-products from shale commercially, at a cost approximating that of oil and its byproducts obtained from wells.'

"No one can even approximate such a process without knowing characteristics of the shale to be used, the products desired, and the cost of oil from wells, that is the real cost, not the mere maintenance of a flowing well, but the cost of getting an average gallon of oil from oil wells, including all dry holes and all preliminary expenses.

"We have produced several thousand gallons of oil and are improving each run, but there is much research work to be done, and if people would devote part of the energy wasted in stock jobbing, the actual research work it seems quite likely the shale oil business would cease to be a by-word. So far as I can see most of the newspaper 'ads' are either based on misinformation or are given out to sell shares. What is the use in publishing (what is very possibly a fact) that the Government estimates the oil shale of Colorado, Utah, Nevada to contain fourteen times as much oil as man has ever taken from the oil wells. What of it, unless somebody finds a way to make it available. It is probably equally true that the waters of the sea contain over a thousand times more gold than man has ever found on the land, but also what of it, so long as nobody does anything.

"Instead of giving money to stock-jobbing pirates who do no actual work with it, if people could honestly expend even a small portion of the money so wasted, in actual research work one might expect very interesting results."

J. B. Mull[184] summarized the operations of the second retort as follows:

"By the end of 1919, this new retort had produced about 15,000 gallons of crude oil. After extended experimentation with it, Mr. Catlin decided to abandon work on it in favor of a larger but less complicated unit, often described as a 'gas producer' or 'blast furnace' type."

Precisely when the second retort was shut down and abandoned cannot be determined from the record. J. B. Mull[185] estimated work was terminated between September 1919 and September 1920, for he asserted: "When I arrived in 1922, it had not been heated for two or three years."

J. B. Mull[186] also described the third retort (Fig 49) and its operation as follows:

"The third and last large-scale retort built at Elko was a steel cylinder about 40 feet high and about 12½ feet in diameter (square at the grate level). The lower section of the retort was lined with firebrick. Raw shale was charged into the top of this unit periodically by manual operation of a bell-valve.

"The spent shale was discharged into a concrete ash pit beneath the retort by hydraulically operated grates. Fixed carbon in the spent shale was burned in a fire zone immediately below the retorting level. The burning was controlled by recycle blowers which returned a mixture of air and boiler stack gases into the ash pit beneath the grates. Oil vapors and gases were drawn from the top of the retort through a series of air- and water-cooled condensers and an electrostatic precipitator after which the uncondensable gases were burned under the plant boilers providing process steam for the retorting and refining departments."

Mull[187] summarized the operation of this retort as follows:

"This retort was placed in operation in December 1921, and operated intermittently until the plant shut down permanently on October 18, 1924. During the final 10 months of operation, four runs for a total of 198 operating days produced 9,095 barrels of crude oil, averaging 46 barrels of oil per day from 77 tons of shale, per stream day. During the final year the mechanical operation of

Fig. 49—View of Catlin Shale Products Company, Elko, Nevada, about 1923. (Source unknown.)

the retort was quite satisfactory. More than once, shutdown of the retort was caused only by full crude oil storage tanks. The refinery capacity was not large enough to keep up with the improved retort production.''

At about the time (1924) the plant was permanently closed, Sheeler[188] wrote to Wadleigh:

"We are putting our products on the market, and have sent a car load of paraffine to the Orient and are making some headway in establishing a market for our lubricant oils . . . We have accomplished what we started to do, namely, to develop a retort to treat shale in mass and sell the finished products to the people that stands up with other competitive products. Our particular lubricants are superior to any on the market.

"You hear of so many other processes and of cheaper operations; however, the cost of operation on a laboratory scale without actually putting out the finished product is largely a state of mind. We have come through the experimental stage and know that the experimental plant in many cases does not bring the same results that the commercial plant does.''

From the bulk of the evidence, it is clear that Catlin, his staff and others considered the operation to be in the experimental stage, from the beginning to about July 1922 in some instances and beyond in others. For example, the 1919 and 1922 reports filed by the company pursuant to Nevada law with the State Inspector of Mines asserted that the work being conducted was

experimental. The 1923 and 1924 company reports did not include the word "experimental". The 1919, 1922 and 1924 reports were signed by W. L. Sheeler, Superintendent, whereas the 1923 report was signed by Albert E. Thomas, Secretary.[189]

Catlin in an October 1922 letter stated:[190]

". . . I would say that we have been making changes and are still more-or-less in the experimental stage although we have made considerable oil we have not entered the market, nor do we intend to do so until we have passed the experimental stage. . . . We hope in the near future that we will be able to definitely state that we have passed the experimental stage.''

The products finally selected for production were wax (15% of the crude shale oil), gasoline or naphtha (5%), distillate fuel oil (41%) and lubricating oil (14%). The balance was made up of coke and refinery losses.[191] The Consolidated Copper Company of McGill, Nevada, determined as late as July 12, 1924, that the various grades of Catlin oil were unsatisfactory for flotation use.[192]

The trials and tribulations in marketing tests of Catlin shale oil products were numerous and would require considerable space to detail. A summary of this phase of the operations, however, should help explain the closing of the operation in late 1924.

Wax. Catlin's wax product was not acceptable to explosives companies and probably had quality defects that would have made it generally unacceptable, although some was sold.[193] However, wax sales could not support his operation; initiating an industrial operation would not have been justified with wax as its major basis because the demand was decreasing and over-production would have depressed the price.[194]

Gasoline. Catlin's gasoline recovery was very low, and the product was of poor quality. To use it in automobiles locally, it had to be blended with imported casing head gas.[195]

Distillate. The kerosene would not meet Government specifications, and consequently was mixed with the overall distillate product. This could be disposed of only locally for use in commercial engines, and was not acceptable as an engine distillate in California. Transportation costs and low quality precluded its use other than to a limited, local extent.[196]

Lubricating Oil. Catlin's lubricating oil was of too low viscosity to meet specifications. Although performing satisfactorily in some automobile engines, it was unacceptable or even dangerous in others.[197] The results of tests by the U.S. Navy were not encouraging.[198] The U.S. Bureau of Standard's tests revealed that it had no qualities superior to any other low viscosity lubricating oil.[199] Catlin determined from actual market exposure tests that it could not be sold in quantity in competition with eastern lubricating oils, and that to decrease the price in any attempt to do so would have been financially disastrous.[200]

The Catlin Shale Products Company had as its purpose experimentation to devise methods to mine, mill and retort oil shale; to refine the crude shale to produce products similar in quality to petroleum products; and to test the market to determine if the products would compete in quality and price with petroleum products.

While Catlin's final retorting process by mid-1924 had reached operating posture, still the retort had at least one technical problem, that of exploding internally.[201] Mining of oil shale had presented no unusual problems; only the matter of cost was of concern. In any event, it could be said that the first objectives of Catlin had been achieved. The production of quality products and marketing of the products produced was not achieved.

According to reports filed with the Nevada State Mine Inspector, work stopped at the plant in November 1924.[202] Sales thereafter were of a salvage or "wind-up" nature.[203] Figure 50 and Figure 51 show the plant site as it appeared in 1978.

The Catlin experience stands as a unique occurrence in the oil shale history of this country. First of all, it was well financed. Secondly, the capital was furnished mainly by Catlin himself, and his company raised no money through the public sale of capital stock.[204] Thirdly, the project was an integrated operation, embracing experiments on and performance of mining, crushing, conveying, retorting, refining, spent shale disposal and marketing. Finally, and what marked it as absolutely unique, it was the pioneer effort in this country to work out methods to try to produce marketable products from western oil shales which would compete in quality and price with petroleum products.

The Catlin Shale Products Company was dissolved on December 23, 1930. Its remaining assets, estimated by the company "not to exceed $3,716.80", were assigned to Catlin. On January 14, 1931, Catlin assigned his interest in the land and assets to his son, Robert M. Catlin, Jr.[205]

Southern Pacific Railroad Co., Inc.

The Southern Pacific Railroad Company constructed a Pumpherston Scotch retort near Elko, Nevada, in 1919 (Fig 52). One bench of four retorts was built and a trial run made in the fall of 1919.[206]

This retort was located 1 mile east of Elko and about 3 miles from one source of oil shale and about 1.5 miles from another source. There is no oil shale source at the plant site.

The oil shale deposits in the vicinity of Elko were described as follows:[207]

> "In the vicinity of Elko, Nevada, on the Southern Pacific Railroad, there are several small deposits of oil shale of Miocene age. These deposits have been studied in considerable detail, and a number of beds of oil shale ranging in thickness from 2 to 6 feet or more and yielding 50 to 70 gallons to the ton have been recognized. These beds are not only faulted and in places inclined 30 degrees from the horizontal, but they also show great lateral variations in richness. Oil shale from these deposits is being mined and retorted, and the product is being refined, but as yet the plant is operating only on an experimental basis."

This operation was described by Gavin[208] as follows:

> "In 1920, a four-retort experimental Pumpherston unit was erected near Elko, Nevada, by a private corporation, with which the Bureau of Mines cooperated to the extent of assigning one of its consulting engineers (Dr. David T. Day) to

Fig. 50—*View of Catlin Shale Products Company's plant site, Elko Nevada.* (1978 *photograph by author.*)

Fig. 51—*View of Catlin Shale Products Company's plant site. Note city of Elko, Nevada, in background.* (1978 *photograph by author.*)

Fig. 52—*Pumpherston retort and plant of the Southern Pacific Railroad Co. Inc., near Elko, Nevada.* (*Source of photograph unknown.*)

direct the construction and operation of the plant. Although the retorts were built in accordance with plans obtained from Scotland, the brick portions cracked and pulled apart so badly when first heated that repairs would have involved the practical demolition and reconstruction of the plant. The failure probably was due either to unsuitable materials of construction or to too rapid heating of the newly constructed retort. Scotch operators stress the necessity of using specially selected fireclay in the manufacture of retort bricks, and in building the brick parts of the retort. They also emphasize the danger to the brick-work if the retorts are heated too rapidly when first put into operation, or after they have been down for repair. The failure of the Elko plant, however, should not be taken as indicating the unsuitability of the Scotch retort for the treatment of American shales.''

V. C. Alderson[209] described this operation as follows:

"The plant at Elko, Nevada, was erected by the Southern Pacific Company under the general supervision of the United States Bureau of Mines and the personal direction of Dr. David T. Day, of the Bureau. Dr. Day secured drawings of a Pumpherston retort from Scotland and erected a plant one mile east of Elko. The plant consists of a bank of four retorts, each of two sections. The upper one is made of cast iron is fifteen feet high and the lower section of fire brick, twenty feet high. The shale is fed in at the top and in the iron section is subjected to a heat of from 750° to 900°F. Here the oil and gas are distilled. The shale is let down to the lower or fire brick section, where it is subjected to a temperature of 1300°F, or more. Steam is injected and ammonia is produced by the hydrogen in the steam uniting with the nitrogen in the shale. The shale is hauled on trucks from the mine three and one-half miles away. The plant was completed in November 1919, but no reports are available yet.''

C. L. Jones[210] reported on this operation in 1920:

"Acting under the advice of Mr. David T. Day, the Southern Pacific Railroad Company has a complete Pumpherston Scotch retort erected near Elko, Nevada. This plant is well constructed, and follows in detail the specifications of the plans having been secured from that concern. One bench of four retorts was built during 1919, trial run being made in the fall of 1919. This trial run gave poor results, and the writer understands that the officials of the company are thoroughly disgusted with it as an expensive experiment. Two or three facts, however, are obvious on examining the plant:

"(1) The fires were evidently not carefully regulated during the experimental run, as the brickwork is badly burned in places, and had been warped in all four retorts so badly that there is considerable leakage between the upper case iron portion of the retort and the brickwork. While this leakage could no doubt be repaired at small expense, it is not surprising that the trial run gave poor results.
"(2) The plant is poorly located, in that it is nearly a mile from the shale which was to be retorted, and about the same distance from the railroad.
"(3) The shale upon which the test was made seems to be very poor material, and is said to yield only 8 gallons per ton. Commercial yields should not be expected from shale selected at random.''

"This writer believes that results of value would be obtained by operating this plant on a richer shale from a known source, in such a way as to definitely establish the practicability or impracticability of retorting American shales in the Scotch retort. So far as can be ascertained, the trial which was made established neither.''

In December 1919 the following was stated regarding this retort operation:[211] "... While operating there this retort has produced only about two barrels of oil per twenty-four hours, when if extraction had been proper it should have produced at least twenty barrels.'' A September 1920 report was as follows:[212]

"... Plant idle practically all of this year (1920), perhaps from unsatisfactory shale, failure of mechanism to function, or disappointment as to results compared with expectation. Approximate investment $400,000.''

Records of oil production by this operation were not noted in the literature, but it appears that it probably was limited to a few barrels. In December 1921 a news article in the *Salt Lake City Tribune* reported that the Southern Pacific Railroad Company's retort had been purchased by the Catlin Shale Products Company of Elko. Records regarding the Catlin operation near Elko, Nevada, indicate, however, that only lumber, piping and so on, were purchased. This plant did not operate after 1921 and was eventually demolished by the owners.

UTAH ACTIVITIES

Figure 53 shows the site of the Mormon retort and the city of Vernal. Figure 54 shows the location of the

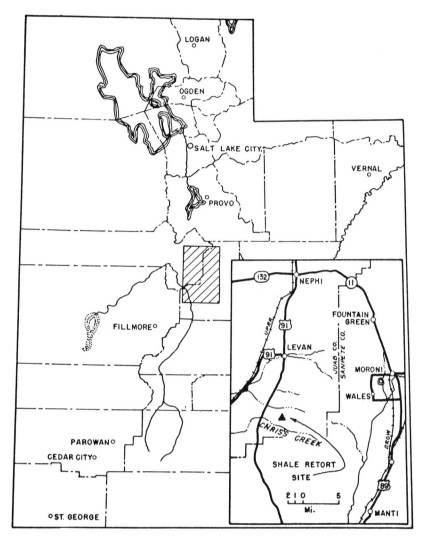

Fig. 53—Utah location map showing site of the "Mormon" retort and the city of Vernal. (From Utah Geological Survey Circular No. 41.)

oil shale operations in the vicinity of the White River and on Willow Creek, all generally south of Vernal. The location of the De Brey retort is not known.

Rocky Mountain Refining Company

(De Brey Retort) A Utah Corporation.

Organized	:	Unknown
Capitalized	:	$50,000
President	:	S. A. Mock—Salt Lake City & Glenwood Springs(?)
Vice-President	:	Unknown
Secretary	:	Unknown
Treasurer	:	Unknown

Property	:	Kyune Canyon, Utah
Location	:	Kyune Canyon
Plant	:	Small plant in Kyune Canyon east of Colton, Utah
Mine	:	Unknown
Production	:	Unknown

Several items in the literature apparently referred to this Utah operation. A retorting process was listed variously as "De Bray", "De Brey", "De Bry" and "Debray". There seems little question that De Brey and De Bray were used to describe the same operation. "De Bry" may have been unrelated to the others. Available information is presented because the literature does

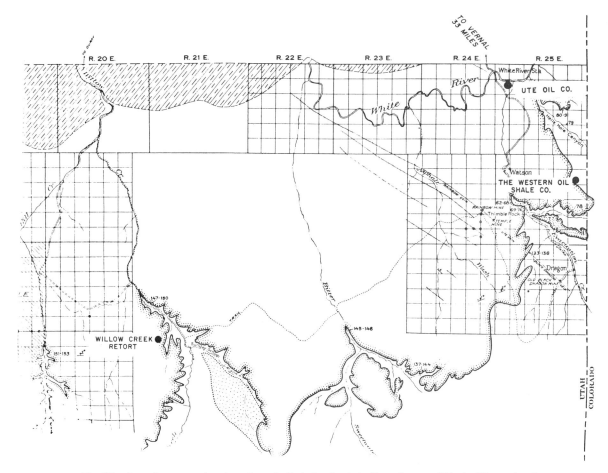

Fig. 54—Location map showing sites of oil shale plants in Vernal area of Utah. (By author.)

report that a retort was constructed in Utah and that it was destroyed by a cloudburst.

Ralph H. McKee[213] describes the De Brey retort as follows:

"The De Brey retort consists of a vertical iron cylinder, about 12 feet in height, in which there is an inner core for the injection of steam. The retort is heated by burning oil shale in two small furnaces on the sides of it. Oil shale is fed in at the top and spent shale is removed directly through a water-seal at the bottom."

C. L. Jones in his report to the Mellon Institute in 1920, listed the De Bray process as being owned by the Industrial Process Company, Salt Lake City, Utah, and adds the comment "Promotion Scheme."

The picture is somewhat confused by the following by H. L. Wood, *National Petroleum News,* July 1920:

"Litchliter, Winter, Sundberg, a partnership operated on its own funds, Mr. Winter having formulated a process that is being modified by

Alvin F. Sundberg with the De Bry French process as a basis, which uses a catalytic agent as a stabilizer of gases. Plant at Salt Lake City nearing completion as a three way retort with warm heat conveyers having vents for gas between each shale container. Intended as testing plant for the shale trade, and the firm will put up a plant in Salina Canyon, southern Utah, to process its own ore. Constructor Sundberg has had experience in shale retorting in Scotland, France, Germany and Austria, besides mining experience in Nevada and mineralogical instructor in University of Utah."

The descriptions of the De Brey retort and the De Bry retort are very different, as is the planned location for the De Bry and the site where the De Brey was constructed. However, there is no record that a retort was constructed in Salina Canyon nor a record that the retort destroyed by a flash flood in Kyune Canyon was ever rebuilt. No records of production by the Kyune Canyon retort were found.

The "Mormon" Retort, Juab County, Utah

This oil shale retort played no part in the effort to develop western oil shales. Indeed, it has been very difficult to establish any facts about the retort other than that it was built and apparently produced some oil; but when it was constructed and by whom seems to have been lost in time.

Dean Winchester reported having seen this retort in 1916, and a photograph he took (Fig 55) has been about the only record available for many years. However, in 1961 the Utah Geological and Mineralogical Survey published[214] the results of a very detailed investigation regarding the history of the retort. Its mention by Winchester and the apparent time of construction and use make this retort very much a part of the history of oil shale in the United States.

All of the information presented here has been abstracted from the Utah publication. Only the highlights are noted, and those wishing more details are recommended to obtain the Utah publication.

Winchester[215] reported in 1916, "Before petroleum was discovered in Pennsylvania, the Mormons distilled oil from shale near Juab, Utah, where the ruins of an old still can yet be seen." [A picture of a retort was shown.]

There is little doubt that this was the first oil shale retort constructed in Utah. Alma C. Dalby of Levan remembered seeing the original retort about 1898. Circumstantial evidence indicates that the retort was constructed after the discovery (1854) of coal at Wales, Utah, and before the outbreak (1865) of the Black Hawk War. Hence, Winchester's off-hand statement probably was founded upon accurate information, though it is now little more than a legend.

In a copyrighted booklet by J. B. Jenson, published in February 1921, the same photograph used by Winchester had "*Salt Lake Mining Review*" written across its face. Underneath the picture is the explanation, "Old Mormon retort near Juab, Utah, used by the Mormons 50 years ago."

Both Winchester and Jenson are irritatingly vague in their references to this pioneer "retort".

After making the point that the retorting of oil shale was not new, Jenson said: "Lubricating oil was also produced from western shales in limited quantities in early history of Utah. An old retort used for this purpose is still in existence near Juab, Utah."

Similar statements in contemporary literature, all later than 1916, appear to have relied either upon Winchester or Jenson for their authority. Circular 41 con-

Fig. 55—Photograph of the Mormon retort taken by Dean Winchester, U.S. Geological Survey, 1916. (From U.S. Geological Survey.)

tinues: "I, [A. L. Crawford], have endeavored diligently, but thus far unsuccessfully, to find some pre-existing records from which these statements could have been drawn."

Because Jenson, a native Utahan, gave no credit for the source of the photograph of the retort and because *"Salt Lake Mining Review"* was printed across the face of the picture, it was first supposed that Jenson, or both Jenson and Winchester, had reproduced an older photograph belonging to the *Salt Lake Mining Review*. No evidence was found to substantiate either theory. After extensive inquiry through the U.S. Geological Survey, Elizabeth Wellshear, Librarian, Denver Branch, found the original negative. It was in the Photographic Library and Field Records File collection of D. E. Winchester's material on Utah. She also found Winchester's supplemental diagram, with his longhand original notes describing the retort he had photographed "in Chris's Creek Canyon", southeast of Juab, September 1916.

The discovery of Winchester's original negatives, field notes and sketches in the archives of the U.S. Geological Survey establishes the retort site as being in the drainage of Chris's Creek, about 5 miles south-southeast of Levan, Utah. On September 3, 1960, the remains of the old retort photographed by Winchester were positively identified and photographed in Shale Hollow, a south-draining strike ravine entering Chris's Creek a few hundred feet east of the Salt Lake Meridan.

Efforts to further substantiate the legend through a preliminary search of the records of the Utah Historical Society, the Latter Day Saints Church Archives and the University of Utah Library thus far have been disappointing.

Dr. Clyde T. Hardy who investigated the geology and has published on this area reported he has heard no local stories bearing on the subject.

It was found that Mr. Alma C. Dalby, living in Levan, Utah, might have traditional evidence that might substantiate existence of this retort. Arrangements were made with Sylvester Pierce, Ernest Pierce and Mr. Dalby to visit the area of Chris's Creek where the retort was thought to be located.

Dalby's story is that in about 1898, he visited, with his father, a north tributary on Chris's Creek in which at that time he had seen an old abandoned oil shale retort that was the subject of discussion between his father and Steve Moss, an old and respected pioneer of the area. Dalby remembers well the story Steve Moss told his father, but has forgotten the names of the

original owners of the retort and other factual data that would enable us to "pin down" the actual history of experimentation. According to Dalby, Moss told Dalby's father that the retort was built by an old pioneer experimenter who extracted as much as a barrel of oil per day. This oil was used as a dressing for harnesses and other leather goods, as a lubricant and as a fuel for wicks in crude illuminating lamps.

At Chases' Ranch, Roy Chase, after viewing the Winchester photograph, stated that this was the retort he had seen in about 1930 when herding cattle in the area. He said he did not remember having seen it when, as a boy, he was in the same area about 1912.

"We found and photographed the remains of the old retort featured by Winchester. There is no question about its identity. The cast-iron floor, headplate, and steel press screw, the scattered brick from the walls of the still shown in Winchester's picture, the old smoke stack, the knucklejoint of the pipes shown in Winchester's photograph, the steel hoops from the barrel used to collect the condensate, charred fragments of the barrel stays, broken fragments of the thick-walled glass tubing used as part of the conduits for the volatile liquids and gases were found either at the immediate site or a short distance down the ravine where floods and men had carried them. The sagebrush, scrub oak, and other vegetation shown in Winchester's picture fit exactly the flora of the location we found and photographed.

"There remains now but to prove that the retort photographed by Winchester was built by Mormon pioneers and was used back as far as claimed by Winchester and Jenson for distilling oil from the kerogen shales of the Green River formation. Such proof may never be found. The trail may be too cold; but the Mormons were record-keeping people, and it is entirely possible that buried in the old records of Juab County, the archives of the L.D.S. Church, or in the obscure entries of the pioneer issues of the *Desert News* is a note that will give the background for this early adventure."[214]

So ends the summary of A. L. Crawford's report of his efforts to solve the mystery of the "Mormon" oil shale retort. He achieved one major objective. He proved that the retort did exist in the area where it was reported. He was unable to determine when or by whom it was built and operated. As time passes, it seems less and less likely that any answers to such questions ever will be found. As A. L. Crawford noted, the "trail may be too cold", but his efforts to resolve this mystery were excellent and thorough.

The author checked with the Utah Geological and Mineralogical Survey in February 1979 to find if any additional information had been discovered. Mr. A. L. Crawford, now retired, was consulted, and he advised that no additional information has been found to add to that published in 1961.

As previously stated, the information presented is a summary of the information contained in circular 41. Reading of the entire report is recommended.*

The Ute Oil Company

Organized	:	1917(?)
Capitalized	:	$1,000,000 par value, $1.00 per share
President	:	J. J. Koenigsmark
Vice-President	:	S. P. Barron
Treasurer	:	A. J. Koenigsmark
Property	:	10,900 acres
Location	:	14 miles from Watson, Utah
Plant	:	Wallace retort never completed
Mine	:	None
Production	:	None

Construction of The Ute Oil Company plant may have started as early as 1917. In 1919 the plans and work were described as follows:[216]

"This company is erecting a 400-ton shale oil plant about eight miles from Watson, Utah on the White River. This is the largest shale-retorting plant under construction in this country. The Wallace process is used. The decision to erect the new plant was based on the results of extensive testing of many samples of shale. The site of the new plant was carefully considered with regard to the availability and delivery of the shale, and the disposal of the residue. The deposit is in the form of a long, high bluff, with no overburden. The mining consists of drilling and blasting down a supply of shale once or twice a week. The shale is then broken by hand to 10 by 15-inch size, and delivered to a 48-in. American pulverizer of ring and hammer type, capable of receiving a piece as large as 15 x 45 in., and crushing to ½ inch with 20% fines and 10% over ½ inch, with a capacity

of 50 tons per hour. The crushed material will be delivered, by an endless belt conveyor, to shale storage bins. From the bins the material will be received by lorries, three in number, running on separate monorails. Each lorry will serve six retorts. The oil from the retort will be conducted through condensers and washers into a large crude-oil storage tank. Each retort holds one ton of shale. It is claimed that the process will extract 90% of the total available oil in one hour. Shale from this locality yields an average of 54 gal. of oil per ton of shale retorted. The lowest yield is 31.5 gal. and the highest 80.5 gal. per ton. It is estimated that the shale, retorted, will yield about one barrel of oil per ton."

The *Railroad Red Book* for January 1920 estimated the cost of this installation at $350,000 and stated that installation was nearly complete and that operations would begin in the early spring. Figure 56 shows the retort being constructed. Construction did not go smoothly and in September 1920 it was reported:[217]

"... A boiler which got away while being lowered to the river level wrecking part of the retorting plant and the repair work not yet completed. Delays in receiving material are holding back work with little having been done this year (1920). It is believed that approximately $400,000 has been spent so far.... Camp buildings will accommodate nearly a hundred people, but the location is somewhat isolated. With completion of the Uintah Railway thru the property next year conditions will be improved materially."

A letter from George E. Cory, Secretary, The Ute Oil Company, to the Texas Company on September 30, 1921, elaborated on the statement above regarding delays in receiving material as follows:

"During the latter part of war we were practically compelled to cease building operations in as much as we were considered non-essential industry and our inability to secure steel and railway transportation during 1920."

C. L. Jones[218] provided the best commentary on these operations in his October 1920 report:

"The only commercial plant of the Wallace process in the United States . . . was constructed by The Ute Oil Co., made up of St. Louis men, at a location 15 miles north of Watson, Utah, on the banks of the White River. This plant is remote from transportation at the present time, but will be within two miles of the extension of the Uintah Railway which is to be built during the coming

---

Note: According to the topographic map of the U.S. Geological Survey Chriss Creek should be spelled with a double "s". However, the spelling Chris's Creek is used throughout Utah Circular 41, and has been used here.

Fig. 56—Wallace retort of The Ute Oil Company, near Vernal, Utah, about 1919. (From Bureau of Land Management, Vernal, Utah.)

year. At the present time the plant is nearing completion, the retort settings and the main structure being complete, although the retorts are not in place, and the condensing and steam-making equipment is not installed. About $100,000 has been expended to date, and it is understood that the work has been halted on account of internal dissentions, it being claimed that A. J. Koenigsmark, a St. Louis banker who provided a large proportion of the money so far invested, will advance no more until given control. It is claimed, however, that the plant will be completed during the summer of 1920.

". . . No shale working has been opened up as yet, and it is believed that surface quarrying is contemplated along the richest ledges until the plant can be gotten well started. An aerial tramway is planned, some of the piers for which have been put in place, but it is not evident from construction now finished just what sort of shale storage is to be provided at the retort site. An impact crusher made by American Pulverizer Co. of St. Louis is on the ground.

"A rectangular bench of 18 retorts has been built, which are arranged in three rows of six each. Over each of these three rows is a beam carrying a running hopper, which is filled with shale and pushed to the desired position in order to charge the retorts. Chain hoists (hand operated) are provided for removing the retort lids. The retorts are of cast iron, and are about 9 ft. long by 2 ft. in diameter. The central perforated take-off is 12-in. in diameter, leaving a 6 in. layer of shale to be carbonized. The lower lids are fastened to each retort by means of four wing nuts. Beneath the bench a track is provided upon which a travelling platform runs. This platform is used by the laborer who opens the retort preparatory to drawing a charge. Upon another track parallel to this one runs a specially designed car for the removal and replacement of the central take-off pipes, which frequently become clogged. Below this runs a link-belt conveyor 24 in. by 40 ft. which carries the spent shale to the dump. The bench of retorts is heated from a firebox placed to one side of the bench, and equipped so that oil, gas, coal, or shale may be burned. . . .

"In operation the temperature of the fire chamber is maintained at about 1400°F., and the retorts are charged intermittently, dropping the

Fig. 57—Oil shale outcrop along tramway of The Ute Oil Company. Note old plant site in upper left and White River in lower section. (From Bureau of Land Management, Vernal, Utah.)

Fig. 58—Remains of plant site of The Ute Oil Company showing old boiler and foundations, 1973. (From Bureau of Land Management, Vernal, Utah.)

old charge out of the bottom, cleaning off the take-off pipe, and charging cold shale from above. This work is done by hand.

"The condensing equipment is not in place, and hence nothing is known of its design. No refining equipment is in place, although a second hand agitator and several small stills are on the ground. Foundations are completed, however, for both condenser housing and for a small room which is apparently intended for refining. Two boilers are on the ground. . . .

"Valuable criticism of such a plant must await some attempt to operate it. However, it may be said that this plant is constructed in more permanent fashion and in accordance with better practice than any other in the west unless it be the Pumpherston and Catlin plants in Elko, Nevada. Two or three points appear to be rather poorly designed, i.e.:

"(1) The retort bench is heated by means of flue gases entering the middle of one side, and leaving through a chimney centrally located on the other side. This arrangement will result in keeping the retorts at the center of the bench at the highest temperature, and should result in making charging and discharging by schedule difficult or impossible, if it does not make a serious difference in the amount and quality of oil produced by the different retorts.

"(2) The amount of manual labor involved in this type of intermittent charging and discharging appears to be excessive, in view of the fact that only about 1 ton of material is handled in each charge. This operation is repeated every 30 to 60 minutes. For purposes of comparison it may be stated that in the modern by-product coke oven, intermittent charging involves the handling of 12 to 15 ton charges every 16 to 30 hours.

"(3) The thickness of shale carbonized (6 in.) seem to the writer to be excessive for this type of retort, although greater thicknesses could be economically handled in a longer retort with the assistance of superheated steam."

The progress in completing construction of this retort continued to be delayed and in January 1922 it was reported:[219] ". . . Work has been delayed by a controversy with the Government over title to the land."

Difficulties apparently continued to plague this operation and the plant never was completed nor was any oil ever produced by this company. The efforts of the corporation were not mentioned in the literature research after about 1922. Figure 57 shows the tramway and Figure 58 shows the plant as they appeared in 1973.

The Western Shale Oil Company

Organized	: 1918 or 1919
Capitalized	: Unknown
President	: H. E. Goldsworthy
Vice-President	: C. H. Wilkerson
Superintendent	: F. C. Merrill
Property	: 1,000 acres
Location	: Nine miles from Dragon, Utah
Plant	: Galloupe Retort
Mine	: Open quarry
Production	: Unknown

The operations of The Western Shale Oil Company were described by H. L. Wood as follows:[220]

"Western Shale Oil Company, Grand Junction, Colorado. Plant located four miles east of Ute switch on Uintah railroad between Dragon and Watson, Utah, near Utah-Colorado state line. Began a thirty-day continuous test run on September 19 [1920] with one Galloupe retort capable of passing thru ten tons of crushed shale. Four other retorts are nearly completed and will be put in operation with a 24-hour changing capacity of fifty tons of shale and a rated output of 2,650 gallons of crude oil, or 63 barrels of 42 gallons, the shale used showing 53 gallons of oil per ton, including the water content, which may be variably from three to eight gallons per ton, much of the visible water settling as in crude petroleum. The Western Shale Oil Company is owner of three-quarters of the Galloupe Shale Process Company, and the business of the organization is to produce crude shale oil for sale to refiners and to manufacture and install Galloupe retorts for the trade. It is the intention of the Western Shale Oil Company to put in operation as quickly as possible enough retorts to produce 400 barrels of crude oil every 24 hours. The plant is as ideally located for accessibility and ease of mining and operation as can be desired, the 1,000 acres of shale land running continuously about the plant, being mostly of an undulating surface presenting no obstacles to travel. There is an abundance of scrub cedar and pine on much of the land and a fine but narrow valley in which the living and other buildings are comfortably placed.

"A good road leads to the railroad. The five retorts and all auxiliary mining equipment cost approximately $150,000. The gas engine will furnish power, for approximately ten retorts, the crusher that can handle as many tons of ore as desired, elevators and other equipment. The spent shale drops into the furnace automatically and provides all the fuel required. Seventeen pipe vents receive the gas as it comes off from top to bottom of the vertical steel retort of 24-inch diameter. The gas is driven from the shale by dry heat, forty to sixty minutes at 750 to 1000 degrees, completing the distillation, the process being continuous. The shale can be mined, open quarry, at the rate of ten tons per man, or by the use of electrical shatterers 20 to 30 tons per man. The setup cost per retort for the fifty-ton plant is approximately $1,500 per ton, but additional retorts can be added as needed at much less, each unit of four retorts being installed economicaliy. The first installation cost was met by the private sale of shales of the corporation. Further operations will be self-sustaining and provide for expansion. H. E. Goldsworthy and C. H. Wilkerson are the organizers; F. C. Merrill is general superintendent and C. F. Anderson assistant. J. H. Galloupe, Denver, is designer of the retorting process. The Western Shale Oil Company is the first plant in the country to make a regular and continuous thirty-day run.''

This operation was described by Dean Winchester[221] in a May 1921 report as follows:

''The Western Shale Oil Company, Jan. 1, 1920,

Fig. 59—Battery of four Galloupe retorts near completion at point of The Western Shale Oil Company, near Dragon, Utah. (From The Shale Review, *January, 1921.)*

Fig. 60—Retort of The Western Shale Oil Company near Dragon, Utah. (From The Shale Review, *September,* 1920.)

Fig. 61—Camp of The Western Shale Oil Company, near Dragon, Utah. (From The Shale Review, *December,* 1920.)

Fig. 62—Ruins of plant of The Western Shale Oil Company, near Dragon, Utah, 1973. (*From Bureau of Land Management, Vernal, Utah.*)

Fig. 63—*Retort on Willow Creek, southwest of Vernal, Utah. Note shaft on left of retort to drive mechanism on top; also remains of building lower right. (1978 photograph by author.)*

completed a single unit Galloupe retort which had a rated capacity of 16 tons of shale per day on its property 4 miles east of Ute Switch on the Uintah Railway near Watson [Utah]. Late in 1920, the condensor house of this plant was destroyed by fire but the construction of a bench of 4 retorts was well along at the time so that the operation of the plant was interrupted only temporarily."

The Galloupe retort used in this operation (Figs 59 and 60) is the same as the retort described in detail in the section on the Dillon, Montana, oil shale operation. In 1922, a report on this operation was as follows:[222]

"The Western Oil Shale Company has completed, on its property nine miles from Dragon Station, four ten-ton retorts of the Galloupe type. Here the retort is adjacent to a solid hill of oil shale so that mining costs will be at a minimum."

Figure 61 shows the camp of The Western Shale Oil Company.

No records of production were located. From the spent shale and other visible conditions, it would appear that production of oil was small, probably somewhere between 5 and 25 barrels. Figure 62 shows the plant area as it appeared in 1973.

There was no further mention of this plant in the literature after 1922.

Willow Creek Retort

The retort on Willow Creek south of Vernal, Utah, seems to be somewhat of a mystery. The only reference to this retort in the literature research was the following:[223]

"J. H. Galloupe is erecting a retort in the Willow Creek district, forty miles west of Watson [Utah], for eastern interests."

It is believed the retort was erected in about 1919 and because of its remote location, it is in a remarkable state of preservation. The retort is about 5½ feet in diameter and about 20 feet high, the stone work encasing the metal cylinders is in very good condition. The gear, drive shaft and belt used to rotate the inner cylinder are still in place. The outlets for the vapors are all in place except for one, although the extensions and the header pipe are gone. A small pile of tar sands and a small pile of broken shale lie above and near the retort. A very small pile of retorted shale lies below the retort. Walls of several buildings are in the near vicinity and a cleared area may have been a stable area. The camp was small and must have been considered remote even in its day. Inspection of the retort and the spent shale pile indicates very little operation. In the author's opinion, production could not have been over a few barrels of oil, if that much. Figure 63 and Figure 64 show the retort and retort area as they appeared in 1978. No 1920 pictures were found.

The Galloupe retort is described under the section on the Dillon Oil Company, Montana. The Willow Creek retort apparently was very similar. A picture of the Galloupe retort is shown in the section describing the Western Oil Shale operations in Utah.

The pictures of Willow Creek retort were taken by the author in 1978.

Fig. 64—Galloupe retort on Willow Creek, southwest of Vernal, Utah. John Donnell, U.S. Geological Survey, Denver, provides size comparison. (1978 photograph by author.)

WYOMING ACTIVITIES

In Wyoming, oil shale is confined almost wholly to the Green River Formation, which occurs in the Green River Washakie, Great Divide, Fossil and Red Desert basins, in the southwestern part of the state. Detailed studies have been only in the Green River Basin south of the Union Pacific Railroad, but available data indicate that the oil shale in southwestern Wyoming is in thin beds and that the area underlain by rich deposits is comparatively small.[224]

As in Colorado and Utah, nearly all oil shale outcrops had been covered with claims by 1920. These shales apparently were less attractive than the Utah and Colorado shales, and development was much slower and much less extensive. However, there were some activities.

The Wyoming Oil Products Company

Organized	:	The Wyoming Oil Products Company was incorporated July 2, 1925—State of Wyoming
Capitalized	:	Unknown
President	:	M. L. Rogers
Vice-President	:	L. A. Irwin
Resident Agent	:	James R. LeMarr
Property	:	640 acres
Location	:	About 1½ miles west of Green River, Wyoming
Plant	:	Trumble retort
Mine	:	Underground
Production	:	Unknown

The Wyoming Oil Products Company and The American Shale and Petroleum Company (see later) were apparently among the few Wyoming activities that included mining and/or retorting. Other activities apparently were mostly for the purpose of obtaining oil shale lands for future use. "The shale of The Wyoming Oil Products Company was reported to run 58 to 64 gallons per ton and there were plans to erect an eduction [retorting] plant in the spring."[225]

A 1927 report[226] described this plant as follows:
"The Wyoming Oil Products Company, has just completed and put into successful operation, a Trumble Plant at Green River, Wyo. It consists of 12 retorts, 600 pound capacity each. The raw material is dumped into bunkers and from there into preheaters. Each preheater is constructed so that the capacity of each one is exactly that of a retort. Hence, when the contents of a preheater are dumped into a retort there is no difficulty about gauging the amount. The preheaters are especially constructed and designed to be heated by the waste flue gases from the boiler and superheater stacks. The temperature of the material dumped into the retorts from the preheaters is as close to 300°F. as it is possible to keep it. The hot products of combustion from the stacks can be by-passed in order to keep the temperature in the preheaters just below the distillation point. The steam from the boiler passes through a superheater and hydrogenator where a portion of the steam is turned into hydrogen, thence to the first retort and from there to the second retort. From this retort, the steam and hydrogen, plus the vapors from the two retorts, pass through a depthlegmator, where the heavy oil or way fraction is trapped off. From there the light vapors, hydrogen and superheated steam, go through another superheater, where the temperature is stepped up to a point approximately 1,200 degrees F., and the same operation is repeated through the 12 retorts. The vapors from the cracking still are also sent down these 12 retorts, the gasoline fraction being taken off at the proper temperature. The plant has operated efficiently and has demonstrated the fact that 12 retorts in a circuit are not too many; in fact, no pressure was lost in operating these 12 retorts, and it is quite possible that another battery of 6 or 12 retorts can be added. The steam necessary to distill the shale in one retort does for the 12 retorts. There is no more steam used in this operation than is necessary to handle one retort. In a large commercial plant, these retorts would be of at least five-ton capacity.

"One of the most interesting and important features developed in the Green River Plant is the fact that heat consumption, after the plant is in operation, is so low that sufficient fixed gas is developed from the distillation to provide all the heat necessary. The production of this gas is not made at the expense of cracking the oil. It is on account of the hydrogenation and vapor phase reactions which take place owing to the fact that the temperature is stepped up and down between 350 degrees and 1,200 degrees F., in the presence of hydrogen, superheated steam, oil vapors and hot carbon, 12 times before the vapors are released. Furthermore, the condensing apparatus is very inexpensive because the vapors are released at low temperatures. This, of course, makes for efficiency as the specific heat is taken out of the steam, oil vapors, and gases in the last retort, helping in the distillation thereof. The daily expected throughput is expected to be close to 70 tons when the plant has become attuned and run steadily."

A report covering the period of October 1, 1926, to September 30, 1928, noted the completion of this plant during 1927, adding, "Extractions as high as 40 gallons of oil per ton are already reported. . . ." Capacity of the plant was reported to be 50 tons per day.

The *Mineral Statistics Report* for the year 1927 listed The Wyoming Oil Products Company. However, the production figures were a total of production from the Bureau of Mines Rulison operation, Rulison, Colorado; Washington Shale Oil & Products Company, De Beque, Colorado; and the N.T.U. Company, Santa Maria, California; and the amounts produced by each entity are not available. The *Mineral Statistics Report* for 1928 did not list The Wyoming Oil Products Company.

Articles of Incorporation for the company were revoked May 15, 1929.[227]

The American Shale and Petroleum Company

C. L. Jones[228] visited The American Shale and Petroleum Company mine near Green River in 1920, and reported as follows:

> "The . . . company of San Francisco have mined out two drifts into the shale on their property near Green River, Wyoming. . . . Two 150 foot entrys, one of which has a twenty-foot raise at its end, have been mined into rather poor looking papery shale, which grows gradually blacker and more massive back from the surface. . . . surface samples yield 7 to 8 gallons per ton . . . samples from the same stratum at the back of the entry yielded 40 gallons per ton.
>
> "In this working, excellent floors and roofs were found, requiring no timbering. The only difficulty . . . great amount of fine dust which interfered with the drill operator, necessitating changing off at this task every two hours."

It was reported that this company owned 1,240 acres of shale land in Sweetwater, Wyoming, and that erection of a Jensen Retort was to begin April 1, 1920. There are no records that this retort ever was constructed.

NEW BRUNSWICK, CANADA, ACTIVITIES

New Brunswick, Canada, is not by any stretch of the imagination, the location of "western oil shales." However, the events described took place during the same time frame, 1915-1930, as those on the western shales. Also the retort constructed there (Fig 65) was one developed for, and used on, western shales. These circumstances led to the decision to include the Canadian activities in this description of western shales.

The New Brunswick area of Canada was the type and principal location for the mineral albertite. This tar-like hydrocarbon was used both in Canada and the United States prior to discovery of natural petroleum in 1859 as a source of both oil and gas. The area became inactive soon after 1859. Interest in oil shales during the post World War I era included renewed interest in New Brunswick.

D'Arcy Exploration Company

The following report of activities was assembled from the general literature and no special effort was made to obtain details of the Canadian operations. The following was abstracted from a book, "Oil Shale" by Ralph McKee, published in 1925:

> "In about 1849 Dr. A. Gesner a local geologist discovered on Frederick's brook in Albert county, a valuable deposit of the mineral which subsequently became known as Albertite. Some fifteen years later (approximately 1860-1864) a number of the oil shale beds were examined and at Baltimore, in Albert county, a retort and stills were erected. This plant treated several thousand tons of shale with the crude oil product being later refined and used generally in New Brunswick and Nova Scotia. The operation ceased soon after petroleum from wells became available. In 1908 a trial shipment of some 45 tons of oil shale was mined near Baltimore and shipped to Scotland for treatment by the Pumpherston Oil Company. A joint company and Canadian Department of Mines report in 1909 showed favorable results. The outbreak of War in 1914 prevented commercial development.
>
> "Representatives of the D'Arcy Exploration Company made a detailed examination of parts of the area and a small retort of the Wallace type, with the necessary condenser, scrubber, pumps, etc., was installed on the west branch of Turtle Creek near the Rosevale Post Office. The retort

Fig. 65—Wallace retort of D'Arcy Exploration Company, near Moncton, New Brunswick, Canada. (From The Shale Review, *November, 1921.)*

had a capacity of 100 lbs. No results of the work are available." [1925.]

The Colorado School of Mines Quarterly for October 1919 reported the following:

"The oil shales of New Brunswick are located in three areas—the Taylorville, Albert mines, and Baltimore. In Taylorville are four beds of shale of good quality; one five feet, one three feet, and two, one foot ten inches thick. In Albert mines are six beds of the following thickness (the most important in New Brunswick): 6.5 feet; 3.5 feet; 5 feet; 4.5 feet; 6 feet; and one with thin beds of oil shale. In Baltimore are four beds 4, 5, 7, and 6 feet thick respectfully."

"Oil Shale", by Ralph McKee, describes the retort used in New Brunswick as follows:

"The Wallace retort at Rosevale, N.B. is 11 ft. high overall, including bottom and top mouth pieces, and takes a charge of oil shale 8 ft. 6 inches high. The cross section of the retort at the center measures 14 inches by 30 inches, the full taper in 11 ft. being 4 inches. The area of the working surface is 63.24 sq. ft., and it said that in excess of 5 lb. of oil shale may be retorted per sq. ft. per hour at a temperature of 1100°F. All the products of distillation are withdrawn inwardly into a central collection chamber, from which they immediately escape. It is stated that the temperature of formation is probably the highest temperature to which any of oil vapors are subjected at any stage of the process of retorting."

The *Railroad Red Book* for January 1922 reported the following:

"According to G. W. Wallace the plant was started April 26 (1921) and has been in continuous operation since that time, making good oil and recovering a full yield."

The *Railroad Red Book* for January 1923 reported as follows:

"The D'Arcy Exploration Company of England erected a Wallace retort near Moncton, New Brunswick and carried on experimental work from April until December (1921). George Howell of London estimates that in New Brunswick, 200 million tons of shale of commercial value will be found, provided successful retorts are designed and working costs are kept down."

No records of operation or production of shale oil from this venture were found.

PART III

1940–1969

Retorting Methods

In order to better understand the progress of current operations, a brief description or definition of the terms "surface retorting", "true in situ retorting", and "modified in situ retorting" may be helpful.

SURFACE RETORTING

Early attempts to recover oil from oil shale utilized some sort of container into which broken particles of shale could be put so that heat could be applied and the oil recovered. Over the years these surface containers or retorts became very complex, and different methods and means for providing the required heat were developed. Oil shale was mined either on the surface or from underground, crushed, and transported to the surface vessels. Retorts were of a "batch" type where the retort was filled, oil recovered, spent shale dumped and the cycle repeated, or the retorts were of a "continuous" type where the shale flowed through the retort, so to speak, with fresh crushed shale being added as retorted or spent shale was removed. Surface retorts today are still operated in this way.

TRUE IN SITU RETORTING

The possibility of retorting the oil shale in place has always been an attractive alternate to mining and surface retorting because it would eliminate mining, crushing and handling as well as the necessity to dispose of spent shale. One common method for true in situ processing of oil shale is to drill a pattern of wells wherein a central well is ringed by four or more production wells. The shale is fractured between the wells by hydraulic pressure (hydrofracturing), or by using explosives, by a combination of both, or by other means. Air is injected into the central well and the shale ignited. The resulting hot gases are forced through the fractures and convert the organic matter into oil, which is pumped to the surface from the surrounding production wells. Hot gases such as meth-

ane, steam, hot liquids or other means may be used to supply heat required rather than the ignition process.

True in situ retorting has not been economically or technically successful to date, although field tests have been conducted during the past 25 years by Sinclair Oil, Equity Oil, Humble Oil, Mobil Oil, Shell Oil, Marathon Oil and by the Federal Government. Tests were conducted in Sweden where electric heaters were inserted into holes drilled into the oil shales, but this did not prove successful.

MODIFIED IN SITU RETORTING

The term "modified in situ" was coined to distinguish this method of recovery from what we now call "true in situ". The true in situ process involves no mining or disposal of mined or retorted shale. Modified in situ involves mining from about 10 percent to 30 percent of the shale to provide the necessary void volume into which the remaining shale is blasted. This produces a room of rubblized shale which allows the passage of the hot retorting gases or liquids. One might envision a vertical or horizontal cylinder where a central opening equal to 10–30 percent of material for any given diameter and length is removed. The area between the outer circumference and the center void is drilled and blasted. The resulting structure filled with broken shale could be an in situ retort. The retort may be square, rectangular or round in cross section and the void space produced by mining prior to blasting may be of any shape and in any location within the structure. The important thing is that void space should be uniformly distributed throughout the broken rock mass so that the heat source contacts as much of the shale as possible during retorting.

Experimental modified in situ retorting was conducted in the Wurttemberg shale fields of Germany during the mid-1940s. Oil yield was reported to be about 30 percent and apparently work was not continued. It is reported that in Estonia (USSR) horizontal retorts were constructed and oil was recovered by in situ retorting. Published information is not available, although it is believed that the work was conducted in the late 1940s or early 1950s.

Occidental Petroleum Corporation began modified in situ field tests in 1972 and has demonstrated a potential for this system. However, as of this date, modified in situ retorting has yet to be demonstrated as technically and economically feasible.

Summary

The current status of oil shale retort development and retorting technology is summarized as follows:

Oil shale processing has been under development in the United States for approximately 60 years without reaching true commercialization. To convert organic material in oil shale into oil and gas the shale generally is heated to about 900°F. Heat may be supplied either by direct heating, utilizing process heat from burning spent shale or part of the product mix, or by indirect heating, utilizing hot gases or hot solids. Important factors are quality of the shale, maximum temperature and quantity of carbonate materials decomposed by the heating. Approximately 600,000 to 800,000 BTU are required to retort one ton of oil shale.

The transfer of heat to the raw oil shale to induce retorting is probably the most important factor in processing of oil shale to produce shale oil. Two basic processes have been utilized in recent years, a direct fired process and an indirect fired process.

In the direct fired process combustion within the retort produces the heat required for the retorting of the raw shale. Retorts using this heating method are the Paraho direct retort, the Union Oil Company A retort, and the Bureau of Mines Gas-Combustion retort. The Nevada-Texas-Utah (N-T-U) retort was the first major direct fired retort and was used extensively by the Bureau of Mines in the 1920s and again in the 1940s. This retort was also used successfully in some foreign production of shale oil. The current modified in situ retorting involves the same concept as used by the N-T-U process.

The indirect heating process includes those processes using hot gas and those using hot solids as a heat carrier. In each case the hot gas or hot solid comes into direct contact with the raw shale to induce retorting. The hot gas concept is utilized in the Paraho indirect concept and in the Union Oil Company B concept. The use of externally heated solids to provide process heat is used in the TOSCO II and in the Lurgi-Ruhrgas processes.

One other process, indirect heating through the wall of the retorting vessel, was used by all western oil shale retorting operations during the 1917–1930 period with one exception: the final and most successful retort operated by the Catlin Shale Products Company, near Elko, Nevada, used a direct fired process.

No retort to date is considered to have demonstrated commercial application. All retorts noted have produced shale oil. Each retort has had advantages and disadvantages both from a technical and economic viewpoint. It seems reasonable to assume that one or more of the retorts noted will become commercial at some future date.

World War II and Post-War Years

All of the early oil shale operations had been abandoned by 1930. Supplies of well oil were plentiful and oil shale interest was at its lowest ebb.

The petroleum shortages of World War II resulted in renewed interest in oil shale. The need to assure oil for future naval needs resulted in the Bureau of Mines resuming research activities that had ceased when the Rulison operation was closed in 1928. There was a renewed interest by the oil industry. Sinclair Research, Incorporated and Shell Oil Company conducted research to determine if shale oil could be produced by methods that did not require mining and surface retorting. Union Oil Company opened a mine similar in design to the Rifle, Colorado, project mine and erected a surface retort. Mining and retorting research was conducted. Nuclear explosives developed during World War II were considered for use in extraction of oil from oil shale and projects were designed, but not carried out. Oil shale research was terminated by the Bureau of Mines in 1956 when the Congress failed to appropriate needed funds. However, the Rifle research facilities were maintained in stand-by condition. These facilities were leased by the Colorado School of Mines Research Foundation and a consortium of oil companies and others conducted mining and retorting research.

While considerable progress was made in developing mining methods and in retort design, the production of shale oil was not great. Union Oil Company produced an estimated 53,000 barrels, the Bureau of Mines produced a few thousand barrels, and Sinclair and Shell Oil each produced a few barrels. The emphasis appeared to be on research, not production.

The post-World War II years are briefly outlined to complete the record up to the current era.

Bureau of Mines, Rifle, Colorado Project

Detailed descriptions of much of the Rifle project are contained in Bulletin 611[229] and in the brochure,

"Oil-Shale Demonstration Plant";[230] both were prepared by the Bureau of Mines and are of public record. Sections from both publications were used in full or abstracted for this section. The author was employed by the Bureau at the Rifle Project and helped to perform much of the research described.

In 1944, while this country was still at war, a group of statesmen foresaw the possibility of an oil shortage in the United States. Demand for petroleum was increasing at an extremely rapid pace while the nation's reserve capacity to produce oil had diminished, and it was becoming increasingly difficult and costly to find new reserves.

These statesmen were aided by many who recognized three facts: (1) that this nation should not depend on foreign oil in an emergency, (2) that the United States contains one of the outstanding oil-shale reserves in the world and has coal reserves of great magnitude, and (3) that American ingenuity could develop better and cheaper methods of producing synthetic liquid fuels than those used in foreign lands.

As a result, the 78th Congress passed Public Law 290, known as the Synthetic Liquid Fuels Act, and it was signed on April 5, 1944. This Act authorized the design, construction and operation of plants to produce synthetic fuels from coal, oil shale, agricultural and forestry products and other substances.

In selecting a site for the oil-shale project, the objective was to find a place that would be typical of those on which commercial projects would be established later. From geological information, it appeared that the Green River formation was the only one likely to become commercially important in the near future. Accordingly, surveys were conducted over the Piceance Creek Basin in northwestern Colorado. Open cut mining was not considered practical, and only regions adaptable to underground mining were considered.

Finally, the Anvil Points area on Naval Reserve land a few miles west of Rifle was selected as the most desirable of 19 possible sites considered for the demonstra-

103

tion plant. The shale was of average quality, the site was well-adapted to a small oil-shale operation, but it was undeveloped in any way.

Construction began in the spring of 1945. Roads and structures were started, and a mine (Fig 66) was opened to supply shale to a retorting plant. Excavation for water and sewer systems was undertaken as well as construction of power and telephone lines. Fifty demountable houses and several plant buildings were moved from a Bureau plant in Kansas and erected on the Rifle site. Before a road from the plant was completed, supplies were packed to the mine on mules, and the miners rode horses to work. Early in the summer of 1945 a portable compressor was pulled up the mountainside by man-power and horses.

Late in 1945 a contract was awarded to the Southwestern Engineering Company of Los Angeles for erection of plant, retorts and supporting facilities. Work was completed in the spring of 1947, and the first batch of shale was retorted on May 8, 1947. Operation of the refinery began on July 11, 1949.

The Rifle project included three major divisions: (1) mining, (2) retorting and (3) refining. The major functions of the mining program were to supply oil shale to the retorts, to devise mining procedures, and to develop an underground mining method by which oil shale could be produced safely and at a low cost per ton.

Experimental mining began in 1944. Mining was conducted using a room-and-pillar method (Fig 67) in which rooms were 60 feet wide and pillars were 60 feet square. A mining height of 50 feet was obtained by removing a 27-foot thickness as an upper heading, then excavating a 23-foot-thick bench. These dimensions later were changed to provide a 39-foot-high upper level with a proposed 34-foot bench. The lower bench was not excavated, although a section of the mine did reach the 50-foot height (Fig 68).

Headings were drilled and blasted using multi-drill jumbos designed just for this purpose. The broken shale was loaded into 12–20 ton trucks using an electric shovel having a 3-cubic-yard dipper. These and other innovations permitted the Bureau to achieve the mining objective of the project and even exceed the goals set at the start of the program. A rate of 148 tons per man-shift underground was attained in test runs at a direct cost of less than $0.30 per ton. The total cost of mining shale, crushing it, and transporting it to the retorting plant was estimated at $0.48 per ton. This estimate includes management, depreciation, taxes and insurance, but no depletion, profit, income taxes or off-site installations (such as power plants, waterworks, and dwellings for workmen). Adding all of these items (including a six percent return on investment), the cost of crushed shale delivered to the retorts would be about $0.75 per ton.

Fig. 66—Anvil Points oil shale mine site of U.S. Bureau of Mines, near Rifle, Colorado. (From U.S. Bureau of Mines.)

Fig. 67—*U.S. Bureau of Mines room-and-pillar oil shale mine near Rifle, Colorado. (From U.S. Bureau of Mines.)*

Fig. 68—*Underground view in Bureau of Mines oil shale mine, near Rifle, Colorado, showing two-level mining.*
(*From U.S. Bureau of Mines.*)

Eight different retorting processes were studied, some foreign and others of United States origin. These processes included: (1) Hayes, (2) flash carbonizer of the Tennessee Valley Authority, (3) N-T-U, (4) Royster, (5) thermal solution, (6) radiant, (7) gas-flow, and (8) gas combustion. In addition, tests were observed on a Union Oil Company continuous, internal-combustion-type retort, and one developed by the Standard Oil Development Company that employed a "fluidized solids technique".

The Bureau selected a Nevada-Texas-Utah (N-T-U) batch retort for basic retorting use while experimenting on retort design. The final product of this research was the development of a "gas combustion retort" (Fig 69) having about a 300-ton-per-day capacity. In this retort, shale moves down through the retorting vessel continuously while gas flows upward through the shale bed. Air is injected in the central portion of the retort, and the gas burns, providing heat for the retorting. Oil and gas driven from the shale by heat are carried from the retort with the gas stream, and the oil is separated from the gas. Part of the gas is recycled through the retort, entering at the bottom, and the remainder is vented. Research was not complete when the facility was closed in 1956.

The experimental shale-oil refinery began operations in July 1949 and demonstrated that gasoline, diesel fuel, distillate fuel oils and heavy fuel oils can be made by thermal processing, followed by acid-treatment and doctor-sweetening of the motor-fuel frac-

Fig. 69—Gas flow retort of U.S. Bureau of Mines, near Rifle Colorado. (From U.S. Bureau of Mines.)

tions. Refinery costs were somewhat higher than for petroleum owing to higher refining losses, but were considered within reason.

A roof fall at the mine occurred in 1955 and prompted the planning of alternate mining methods that would allow the extraction of thick oil-shale beds without the necessity of men and equipment working under a high roof.

All activities at the Rifle project were suspended in 1956 when Congress ceased providing funds for the activity.

The objectives of the project were met for the most part. A mining system at reasonable costs was demonstrated. A continuous retort was developed and demonstrated. Refinery operations showed that shale oil could be used to produce products generally equal to those produced from petroleum. The project did not fully demonstrate commercial production nor determine commercial costs. These functions would have been done by industry. The indicated costs were apparently too high to elicit industry interest; and with natural petroleum still plentiful, the project was closed.

The mine and plant were maintained in standby condition and this facility has been reactivated by industry several times for the purpose of research. (*See* Colorado School of Mines Research Foundation and the Paraho sections of this book.)

Sinclair Research Incorporated

In 1953–54 Sinclair conducted tests to determine whether true in situ recovery of shale oil from Colorado oil shales might prove feasible. Information regarding this work was prepared by Bruce F. Grant, a former Sinclair employee.[231]

Sinclair Oil and Gas Company (now a part of Atlantic Richfield Oil Company) conducted a study on the feasibility of in situ retorting at a site near the southern edge of the Piceance Creek Basin. Wells were drilled into the shale beds and a horizontal fracture or fractures were established between the wells. A propane gas burner was inserted into the injection well and the oil shale ignited. The burning zone was regulated so that the heat flowed by conduction to the nearby shale. The hydrocarbons thus produced were carried by the gaseous combustion products through the fracture system and recovered from nearby producing wells.

From these tests it was concluded that communication between wells could be established through induced and natural fracture systems; that wells could be

ignited successfully although high pressures were required to maintain injection rates during the heating period; and that combustion could be established and maintained in the shale bed. During the 1960s, Sinclair conducted research in the deeper and thicker deposits in the Yellow Creek drainage near the center of the Piceance Creek Basin.

The results of both the 1953–54 and 1960s tests were inconclusive. A few barrels of oil were produced.

There are no available records showing that this area of research was continued after Sinclair became a part of Atlantic Richfield Oil Company.

Union Oil Company of California, Inc.

The Union Oil Company has continued to hold its oil shale properties acquired in the early 1920s in the Parachute Creek area of Colorado.

The company has conducted considerable research over the years. In 1943, Union began research on a unique oil shale retort. A small two-ton-per-day retort was first constructed at its California plant. In the early 1950s, a 30-ton-per-day retort was tested. The retort used a "rock pump" to push the shale upward from the bottom of the retort. This work progressed to the point of a field demonstration of mining and retorting conducted during the middle 1950s. The following has been abstracted from two papers presented by Fred L. Hartley:[232]

> "In terms of Company objectives leading to the initiation of our intensive shale program, three areas were of major interest. The first involved the development and demonstration of a practical method for extracting hydrocarbons from oil shale rock, on a commercially significant scale. The second was concerned with the development and demonstration of a manufacturing procedure for converting raw shale oil into finished petroleum products. In the third, we are seeking to provide engineering and design bases upon which capital requirements and operating costs of a shale oil facility could be reliably estimated. The demonstration plant was located in northwestern Colorado at a point where the east, west, and middle forks of Parachute Creek join to form the main body of the creek.

> "Until October 1957, oil shale for use in the retorting experiment was obtained by surface mining. As this source of shale was exhausted plans were made for an underground mine [Fig 70]. The objectives of our mining research program were

to develop, as necessary, new mining techniques; to supply typical underground oil shale rock for retorting; and to develop a commercial mining configuration, and firm mining costs. Basically, the mine [Fig 71] was patterned after the Bureau of Mines' oil shale mine at Anvil Points, Rifle Project. Rock obtained from this mine was transported first by truck to a primary crusher, and then to the valley floor, eleven hundred feet below, by aerial tram [Fig 72]. The oil shale rock is then selectively fed, on a predetermined size-range basis, into the Union Oil retort. Rock of a major dimension of up to five inches can be easily handled. . . .''

The Union Oil retort (Fig 73) was described by Hartley[232] as follows:

"The operation of this retort is best described as 'continuous, underfeed, counter current retorting'. The fact that crushed shale is fed upward from the bottom of this retort with a ram-like piston serving as a 'rockpump' makes the design unique. [The principal upon which this 'pump' operates is shown in Figure 74]. Here we see the rockpump successfully take on a charge of shale, swing over into the pumping position, pump oil shale rock up into the retort, and then return to the original position, to take on a fresh charge of shale. As the shale rock is pumped upward, it is contacted by the hot gases pulled down past the rock by blowers. These hot gases result from the burning of residual carbon in the oil shale ash at the top of the retort. The oil condenses on the relatively cool incoming rock, and recovered oil and combustion gases are withdrawn from the bottom of the retort. The shale ash continues upward and is spilled over into a chute. . . . The retort was put in operation during March 1957 and reached its design rate of 360 tons per day by early summer. Knowledge gained through our research program has resulted in a series of design modifications, and the development of new operating techniques, which permitted increased through put rates of up to twelve hundred tons of rock per day. Depending upon the richness of the shale, approximately one-half to two-third barrels of liquid oil, per ton of shale charged, has been produced.'' [The retort was on stream about 190 days and over 50,000 barrels of shale oil were produced.]

Fig. 70—View of Union Oil Co. of California, Inc.'s mine, north of Grand Valley, Colorado. (Photograph by author about 1958.)

The retort was considered to be ready for commerical operation.

Refining research was also conducted by Union Oil and Hartley[232] stated:

"Finished petroleum products obtainable from shale oil include gasoline, diesel fuel, jet fuel, and kerosene of high quality. In fact, products from shale oil are indistinguishable from their natural petroleum counterparts. Shale-derived jet and diesel fuels, for example, can be manufactured to meet all known military, as well as commercial aviation, specifications."

The mine and retort were shut down by August 1958. The operation was considered a technical success. However, the demonstration did not result in the development of a commercial shale oil operation. Reports by the Colorado Bureau of Mines[233] show the progression of this operation as follows:

1955—July 24 report: "Office in Grand Valley. Plans to build retort, etc., on Parachute Creek; 3 employees."

1956—July 14 report: "Stearns Rogers [contractor] installing crushers, trams, buildings, retort, etc., 77 men employed. Isbell Construction of Reno has mining contract, built 4½ miles road to mine—had two bad land slides in early spring."

1956—September 30 report: "500,000 tons removed on [from] surface where quarry is going to be. Tested aerial tram."

1956—November 9 report: "Mined by quarry method—trucked to primary crusher—6". Two Bucket Tram, Jig Back type 4½ ton capacity. Retort under construction."

1956—"$200,000 spent."

1957—February 28 report: "Plant expected to go into continuous operation March 6, 1957."

1957—September 25 report: "Isbell—19 men. Exhausted open cut shale. Plan to go underground. Retort down two weeks—Has been very successful. Retort feed 3 to 6 inches. 56 total employees."

1957—December 13 report: "Two adits started November 1, 30 x 30 feet. 750 tons have been run per day through the retort. Buckets on tram make 40 trips per hour [180 tons]."

1958—July 30 report: "Tram broke, damaged buckets, estimated cost $10,000. Bad ground hit in one adit—used for storage. 831 total feet drifting (30 x 30 ft.)."

1958—"Total 1,845 surface, 1,861 underground shifts."

1959—January 27 report: "Closed—3 men. Water coming out of tunnel."

Most of the plant and equipment were removed and neither the plant nor the mine have been active since 1958. Production of shale oil was not noted in the reports available. However, private sources estimate the total shale oil production may have been in excess of 50,000 barrels.

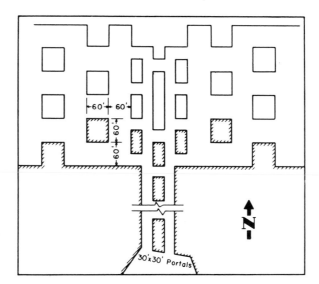

Fig. 71—Proposed layout of Union Oil Co. of California, Inc.'s underground mine, north of Grand Valley, Colorado. (From paper by Fred L. Hartley, 1957.)

Fig. 72—Aerial tramway from oil shale mine depositing raw shale into stockpile for use in Union Oil Co. of California, Inc.'s retort. (Courtesy, Union Oil Co. of California, Inc.)

Fig. 73—View of Union Oil Co. of California, Inc.'s retort at time of dedication in 1957. (Courtesy, Union Oil Co. of California, Inc.)

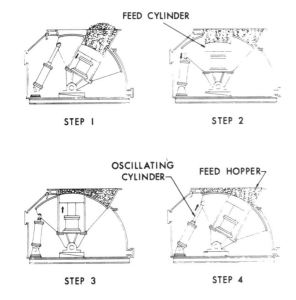

FEED CYLINDER

STEP 1 STEP 2

OSCILLATING CYLINDER   FEED HOPPER

STEP 3 STEP 4

Fig. 74—Union Oil Company of California, Inc.'s "Rock Pump" retort. (From paper by Fred L. Hartley, 1957.)

The Oil Shale Corporation (TOSCO)

The Oil Shale Corporation was organized by H. E. Linden, Beverly Hills, California, as a result of his interest in a Swedish process developed by Aspengren and Company for the pyrolysis of oil shale. He obtained American rights to this Swedish patent that is based upon the use of hot spheres for heating the oil shale to extraction temperatures. Linden began his development of what was to be the TOSCO II process in 1956 and constructed a pilot plant near Littleton, Colorado, in 1957.

In the Tosco II process, crushed oil shale is heated to approximately 900°F by direct contact with heated ceramic balls. At this temperature, the organic material in western oil shale rapidly decomposes to produce hydrocarbon vapor. Cooling of the vapor produces crude shale oil and light hydrocarbon gases.

The thermal decomposition reactions take place in an inert atmosphere in a rotating kiln. The feed streams to the retort are ½-inch diameter ceramic balls heated to about 1100°F and preheated shale crushed to a size consist of ½ inch or smaller. The rotation of the retort mixes the materials and causes a high rate of heat transfer from the ceramic balls to the shale. At the discharge end of the retort the ceramic balls and the shale are at substantially the same temperature and the shale is fully retorted. The balls and the retorted shale flow from the retort into a cylindrical trommel screen. Spent shale passes through the screen openings and into a surge hopper. The ceramic balls flow across the screen and into a bucket elevator for transport to the ball heater where they are heated by direct contact with hot flue gas. The ceramic balls are then recycled to the retort.

The hydrocarbon vapor formed as a result of the retorting reactions flows through a separator to remove entrained solids and then into a fractionation system where the fractions are separated for further processing.

The operations of this company are described further under Current Activities later in this book.

Colorado School of Mines Research Foundation, Inc.

Between 1964 and 1968, the Colorado School of Mines Research Foundation, Inc. leased the Government's oil shale facilities near Rifle, Colorado, as a contractor for six oil companies: Mobil Oil Company (Project Manager), Continental Oil Company, Humble Oil and Refining Company, Pan American Petroleum Company, Phillips Petroleum Company, and Sinclair Research Incorporated (Atlantic Richfield Company). A program was undertaken by the group to conduct research on new mining and retorting techniques.

This venture was started by Mobil Oil Company and was a product of their continuing interest in oil shale that goes back to about 1940. This interest involved research on retorts, and in 1948 Mobil supplied a Congressional Shale Oil Subcommittee with a report on "Design and Cost Estimate for 150,000 Ton Per Day Thermofar Shale Retorting Plant." Mobil worked closely with the Bureau of Mines during the Bureau's 1944–56 operation of the Rifle project. An in-depth study started in 1956 led to further research and in February 1963 the possibility arose that a cooperative research agreement could be made with the Bureau of Mines for use of the facility at Rifle. In July 1963, a new Mobil research group under R. H. Cramer was established for the purpose of studying oil shale technology.

On May 1, 1964, the Colorado School of Mines Research Foundation, Inc. leased the Rifle facilities from the U.S. Government; and Mobil (Socony-Mobil Oil Company, Inc.) contracted with the Colorado School of Mines Research Foundation, Inc. to conduct a research program. Mobil and Humble agreed to supply financing, technical advice and technical manpower, and also agreed to let other interested companies become "Participating Parties".

The express purpose of this operation was to further develop the Bureau of Mines Gas Combustion retort and to operate an experimental mine.

Peter G. Zambas, a Mobil mining engineer, was in charge of the mining research; R. H. Cramer headed the retort research and was the overall manager of the operations for Mobil Oil Company.

The major objective of the mining program was to investigate the technical feasibility of safely mining an 80-foot-thick bed of oil shale at a high rate of production and at a low unit cost. Other objectives included research in all aspects of mining and the production of oil shale as needed for operation of the experimental retorts. All mining production and research was conducted in a new mine opened on property owned by Mobil just west of the main entrance to the Bureau's former production mine.

Large headings (40 x 60 feet) with long 40-foot pillars between rooms, followed by a benching operation, was the general approach for mining. Single blasts broke from 4000 to 9000 tons of shale and demonstrated the stability of the mine. An 80 percent safe extraction within the mining block was projected for an oil shale mine where shale from 75 to 80 foot thick is mined.

The mining research study was considered to be successful, and the mining of oil shale was proven technologically feasible both by the early work of the U.S. Bureau of Mines and by the extensive investigations carried out by the cooperative industry group.

The following information on retort research was abstracted from a paper presented March 1971.[234]

"A number of different methods of retorting have been studied, but only three have progressed to a development stage in the United States. These are the Bureau of Mines downflow Gas Combustion Retort, the Union upflow counter current retort, and the TOSCO heated-ball retort. The Gas Combustion Retort, pioneered at Anvil Points in 1946–56 by the Bureau of Mines, was chosen for the recent further study there. . . . The Gas Combustion Retort is similar in many respects to an iron ore blast furnace. Raw shale, crushed to less than about 3-inch, enters the top of the retort and flows by gravity through the retort and out the bottom. Part of the gas formed in the retorting operation is recycled to the bottom of the retort where it removes heat from the hot retorted shale. As the heated recycle gas flows upward, it is contacted with air and burns along with carbon on the retorted shale, forming a narrow, high-temperature combustion zone across the middle of the retort. The hot combustion gases from this zone continue upward and furnish the heat necessary to decompose and distill the kerogen from the raw shale. The shale oil vapors are cooled by the raw shale in the upper part of the retort and are finally removed from the retort as a fine mist which is separated from the gas by centrifugal collectors and electrostatic precipitators. Dilution gas, either recycle gas or gas from some external source, may be added to the combustion air if required to moderate temperatures in the combustion zone.

"The thrust of the Stage III retort program was to demonstrate scale-up of the Gas Combustion process to a larger size pilot unit and to provide information on which to base design of commercial-size retort elements.

"The runs reported herein demonstrated the capability of scaling-up the Gas Combustion process to a large pilot retort. However, these results were not achieved without difficulty. . . . Also while these runs showed that operability can be achieved under certain conditions, it is currently difficult, if not impossible, to predict what conditions would be required for a commercial-scale operation.

". . . Although specific limits of operability are difficult to state quantitatively, several factors which affect retort operability are enumerated. . . .

"(1) Operation is more difficult on small shale sizes, even when these particles are admixed with larger particles;

"(2) the operation is gas limited; i.e., raising gas rate beyond a certain limit creates poor operability;

"(3) increasing shale rate decreases operability unless compensating changes in gas rates are made; furthermore, operable gas rates and shale are a function of retort hardware; "(4) operations are more difficult on shale assaying greater than 30 gallons per ton.

"For the foregoing reasons, extrapolation of the results presented to encompass widely different operations is extremely risky and not recommended."

The retort work was not a success although the mining operation apparently achieved its objective. All operations were terminated by April of 1968.

Project Bronco

Since the first peaceful detonation of a nuclear explosive in 1957, the possible use of such devices to fracture several million tons of shale at one time has been considered. The ability of the nuclear explosive to break and fracture rock was demonstrated; and in October 1967 a study was made of the feasibility of fracturing oil shale with nuclear explosives and the extraction of oil by in situ retorting. The design of an experiment to test these concepts was prepared by the U.S. Atomic Energy Commission, the U.S. Department of the Interior, CER Geonuclear Corporation, and the Lawrence Radiation Laboratory as PNE-1400

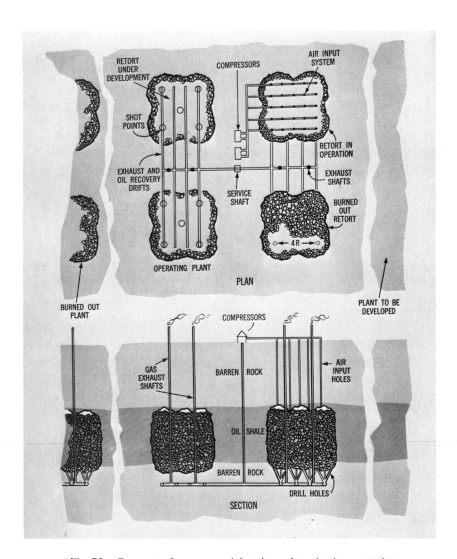

Fig. 75—Concept of a commercial scale nuclear, in situ, retorting plant. (From Report DNE-1400, U.S. Atomic Energy Commission, October, 1967.)

"The Bronco Oil Shale Study."[235] The author, as a Department of Interior representative, participated in this study effort.

The basic objectives of the experiment were:

1. To assess the technical and economic feasibility of in situ retorting as a method for recovering oil from oil shale fragmented and fractured by an underground nuclear explosive.

2. To confirm and refine the capability to predict physical properties and geometry of the cavity, chimney and the fractured region produced by a nuclear explosion in oil shale.

3. To investigate the form and distribution of radioactivity left by the detonation and to assess its effects during in situ retorting.

A site for the proposed test was selected near the southeast corner of Section 15, TIN, R98W, Rio Blanco County, Colorado. The recommended area lies about 1¾ miles west of Core Hole No. 1, drilled by the Bureau of Mines.

It was proposed to use a nuclear explosive of about 50 kilotons energy yield. This yield was large enough so that the cavity created by the explosion would probably collapse, and small enough so that only minimal effects were expected from the seismic wave generated by the explosion. If all went well, the nuclear explosion would have created a rubble-filled chimney 520 feet high with a diameter of about 230 feet. This chimney could have contained as much as 1,150,000 tons of fragmented shale. It was estimated that the detonation would produce fractures in the shale some 460 feet laterally beyond the chimney edge and 700 feet above the shot point. Assuming a 24-gallon-per-ton average grade, the oil content of the rubble chimney alone would have been about 660,000 barrels.

For a number of reasons, Project Bronco was never conducted. A similar project using a nuclear explosive in the oil shales of Utah also was proposed, but it too became involved in problems and was never conducted. Figure 75 shows the concept for a commercial nuclear in situ retorting plant.

Shell Oil Co. Inc.

Shell Oil Company, having started experimental work in 1962, was an early pioneer in attempts to recover oil from oil shale utilizing true in situ processes. This initial work expanded into an extensive geological survey that included drilling, coring and testing of oil shale deposits in Colorado, Utah and Wyoming. Shell employees found that the water-soluble minerals nahcolite ($NaHCO_3$) and dawsonite ($NaAl(OH)_2CO_3$) were mixed throughout much of the oil shale in the deeper central part of the Piceance Basin. It also was recognized that these water-soluble minerals presented a possibility of developing porosity and permeability in the shale beds, if they could be leached and removed. If porosity and permeability could be developed, the oil shale could be heated by steam or some other means and the oil recovered.

Experiments were conducted under extreme secrecy from December 1970 until early 1972 on a small plot of State-owned land along Piceance Creek. Wells were drilled deep into the shale beds to be tested. Cold water was first used for leaching, but hot water was found to leach much faster. A leached zone was formed and permeability established. Steam injected at high pressure into the leached oil shale zone converted the kerogen to oil. The process also continued the leaching of the sodium minerals exposing more shale for oil recovery. There were operational problems and productivity of oil was much below expectation.

Although a detailed technical and economic analysis was difficult, Shell was encouraged. Operations at this site were not resumed, however, and Shell continued its oil shale interest by becoming a partner in the Colorado oil shale lease tract C-b and in the Colony Development Operation. Shell withdrew from these operations in 1974 and has discontinued all oil shale activities for the present.

PART IV

1970–1979

Current Activities

The original intent of this document was to present some of the early history of the attempts to develop western oil shales together with some before and after pictures. Circumstances, however, have once again resulted in interest and optimism that oil shale will yet become a valuable energy resource. The presentation would therefore not be complete without recording the efforts of the new teams of players in the oil shale game and briefly describing their plans and progress. Whatever the results of these new efforts may be, they will have to be reported by some future oil shale buff because many years must pass before an assessment can be made.

GOVERNMENT LEASING

It is estimated that 72 percent of oil shale lands containing nearly 80 percent of the shale oil is Federally owned. Of the higher grade resources, about 81 percent is in Federal ownership. Over the years there have been periods of high interest by industry and individuals in obtaining control of this resource. However, the Federal Government, in keeping with its responsibility to manage all natural resources on Federal lands so that they contribute as effectively as possible to the satisfaction of public needs, has been very successful in resisting such demands. The Tea Pot Dome oil leasing scandal involving public lands in Wyoming may have influenced the Government to exercise caution in deals involving natural resources.

As need for oil shale development increased the Federal Government through the Department of the Interior offered to lease public oil shale lands in 1968. Whether the lease restrictions were too stringent or whether the timing was poor, the total amount bid for the three tracts offered was only $500,000. One bid by Fred C. Crafts, Eugene, Oregon, was 50 cents per acre.

A new offering of oil shale leases was started by the Government in 1971 when an Oil Shale Task Force developed a prototype program and produced a six-volume Environmental Impact Statement. This program offered for lease six experimental sites each of approximately 5,100 acres, two in each of the states of Colorado, Utah and Wyoming. This offering finally came to fruition in 1974. From the Government's viewpoint, the timing could not have been better since it coincided with the Arab oil embargo which had increased petroleum prices sharply. Bid offers for the first tract, designated Colorado C-a, exceeded expectations to such an extent as to be almost unbelievable by those involved. Yet in spite of what was considered to be a very high bid by those knowledgable in oil shales there were charges of "giveaway" and investigations by a Congressional Committee.

The lease tracts were designated C- for Colorado, U-for Utah, and W- for Wyoming with a and b being used to designate number of the tract, that is, C-a; U-b. Fig 2 (p. 4) shows the locations of the lease sites.

Bonus bids were opened on January 8, 1974, for the leasing of Colorado tract C-a and were as follows:

Area: 5089.70 acres. *Oil:* 4.07 Billion barrels (Interior estimate of reserves recoverable by Surface Mining)

Bidder	Bid
1. Standard Oil Company of (Indiana) & Gulf Oil Corporation	$210,305,600.00
2. Sun Oil Company	$175,001,190.98
3. American Petrofina Co., Marathon Oil Co., & Phelps Dodge Corp.	$ 80,000,000.00
4. Atlantic Richfield Co., Ashland Oil Co., Inc., & The Oil Shale Corp.	$ 63,333,333.36
5. Shell Oil Company	$ 63,000,000.00
6. The Carter Oil Company	$ 33,125,294.51
7. Occidental Oil Shale, Inc.	$ 16,361,044.24
Total	$641,126,463.09
Average	$ 91,589,494.72

8. Lawrence S. Shaw, San Diego, California, bid "Forty-nine percent of net profits per acre after production costs. Enclosed find a token payment in the amount of $1 for the bonus bid. If you know the exact amount of this bid I will put up one-fifth of this amount."

The following has been abstracted from a "Special Report" January 10, 1974, by Cameron Engineers, Denver, Colorado.

" 'Never in my wildest dreams did I expect this,' was the reaction by Hank Ash, Deputy Coordinator for the Oil Shale Task Force, to the $210.3 million bonus bid submitted . . . for Colorado oil shale tract C-a. . . .

"To even the most experienced industry veteran of lease sales, this sale must have been as dramatic as any ever attended. The first bid opened was that of Shaw's; it immediately sent whispers of 'farce' through those of the 200 plus people present who remembered the ill-fated lease sale in 1968 when a total of $500,000 was bid for three tracts. But the next bid (by Shell Oil Company for $63 million) quickly dispelled visions of a fiasco and set the stage for the announcement of Gulf and Standard's bid that, for the moment, left the audience in stunned silence. The State BLM official announcing the bids drew in a short breath after opening the Gulf-Standard envelope and hesitated for several seconds to make sure she had the decimal point in the right place—a weaker heart might have fainted. Subsequent audience reaction consisted of various exclamations of disbelief.

"The high bid is equivalent to $41,320 per acre for the 5090 acre tract. Using the estimate given by Interior in the final environmental impact statement for reserves recoverable by surface mining, the Gulf-Standard bid is approximately equivalent to a nickel per barrel.

". . . First, it is obvious that Interior has designed a program that is acceptable to industry. . . . Second, the giveaway aura that has surrounded potential Federal oil shale leasing for the past 10 years has been shattered; the audience at the January 8 lease sale was amused by one reporter who, nonetheless, asked Interior if they expected charges of giveaway." [Such charges were made as mentioned previously.]

There were no surprises in the additional bid offerings that compared with that of the first opening. However, there was decreasing interest that decreased to a point where there were no bids made at all for the Wyoming tracts.

Bids for the second Colorado tract and for the Utah and Wyoming tracts are given in Table IV.

There were other oil shale activities in 1973–74, such as the Paraho retorting operation at the old Bureau of Mines Rifle project site, the Occidental Petroleum modified in situ activities in Logan Wash near De Beque, and the Superior Oil Company exploration and planning efforts on their private holdings in the northern portion of the Piceance Creek Basin.

Lease site activities in 1974–75 were directed primarily at fulfilling the lease requirements for Exploration and Environmental Baseline Data, and at the collecting of a two-year data base. These requirements were completed by the end of 1976. Detailed Development Plans were prepared and submitted to the Area Oil Shale Office, established in June 1974 by the U.S. Geological Survey for the purpose of administering the lease program. Peter A. Rutledge, the Area Oil Shale Supervisor, was headquartered in Grand Junction, Colorado. An Oil Shale Environmental Advisory Panel (OSEAP) was provided for in the Environmental Impact Statement. This Panel was composed of both Government and public members and was for the purpose of assisting the Area Oil Shale Supervisor in administering the extensive environmental requirements set forth in the leases. The OSEAP charter expired in December 1977 and was reactivated on September 19, 1978. Mr. Henry O. Ash, Denver, is the Panel Chairman.

During the first year, environmental data on air quality on all tracts showed that natural background levels of ozone, nonmethane hydrocarbons and particulates on occasion exceeded National Ambient Air Quality Standards. All lessees applied for and were granted a one-year suspension of operations under Section 39 of the Mineral Leasing Act and the Oil Shale Leasing Act. This suspension expired in August 1977 for tracts C-a and C-b, and in October 1977 for Utah tracts U-a and U-b. Air quality standards were modified at about the same time as the expiration of the lease suspensions, permitting work to proceed. In May 1977, lessees of the two Utah tracts filed suit seeking an indefinite suspension of the due diligence requirements and annual bonus payments of the lease until conflicts with regard to overlapping mining claims and State selection of the lease area were resolved. Such suspension was granted in June 1977, and there has been no active development on the Utah tracts since that time.

The 1973 oil embargo turned out to be short-lived, but the cost escalation continued and, as construction costs multiplied, interest in oil shale decreased. In December 1975, Atlantic Richfield and The Oil Shale Corporation withdrew from the C-b lease, and in late 1976 Shell Oil Company withdrew from both C-a lease

TABLE IV

BONUS BIDS FOR LEASING THE SECOND COLORADO TRACT AND FOR THE
UTAH AND WYOMING TRACTS

Date	Tract	Bid	Bidder	1973 estimates of Recoverable Shale Oil
Feb. 12, 1974	C-b	$117,788,000	Atlantic Richfield Ashland Oil Shell Oil The Oil Shale Corp.	723 million bbl. of oil in 30 gal. shale (underground mining)
Feb. 12, 1974	C-b	$52,500,000	Geokinetics Group	
Feb. 12, 1974	C-b	30 cents per barrel royalty	Global Oil Shale Products Co. Redlands, Calif.	
Mar. 12, 1974	U-a	$75,596,800	Sun Oil Co. Phillips Petroleum	331 million bbl. of 30 gal. shale (underground mining)
Mar. 12, 1974	U-a	$25,012,224	Occidental Oil Shale Inc.	
Mar. 12, 1974	U-a	$3,770,000	Geokinetics Group	
Apr. 9, 1974	U-b	$45,107,200	White River Shale Oil Corp.	271 million bbl. of 30 gal. shale (underground mining)
Apr. 9, 1974	U-b	$11,500,000	Geokinetics Group	
May 13, 1974	W-a	—	No bids received	354 million bbl.
June 11, 1974	W-b	—	No bids received	352 million bbl. (Both 20 gal. shale in situ process)

and from the Colony Operation. Ashland Oil, the remaining C-b lessee, announced its partnership with Occidental Petroleum Corporation in late 1976, and indicated that the Occidental in situ technology would be used to develop the tract.

The principal developments during 1976–77 were Paraho's continued work on its contract to produce 100,000 barrels of crude oil for the Navy, and Occidental Petroleum's continued research on its in situ technology at the Logan Wash site. The U.S. Bureau of Mines also let a contract to drill a 10-foot diameter shaft to a depth of about 2400 feet on Government land in Horsedraw, a tributary of Piceance Creek. The Colorado Lessees continued to collect environmental background data and to prepare Detailed Development Plans (DDPs). These DDPs were approved in the fall of 1977, and site preparation was begun on tracts C-a and C-b on the expiration of the suspension granted one year earlier.

Colorado Lease tract, C-a

This oil shale lease tract C-a was first called the Rio Blanco Oil Shale Project, but in January 1978 Standard Oil and Gulf Oil formed a general partnership for development of the lease under the title Rio Blanco Oil Shale Company. This tract was first considered for development as a surface mine with surface retorting, but environmental constraints, including the inability of the company to obtain additional Federal land for offsite disposal of the overburden, caused a change of plans. As revised, the plan now calls for the use of the modified in situ retorting method for shale oil recovery and proposes a four-year modular development phase and a three-year commercial phase. The plan calls for surface on-tract retorting of mine-development materials and on-tract disposal of processed shale and waste materials, with all support facilities also being on-tract. The modular development phase is sched-

Fig. 76—View of Colorado lease site C-a, Piceance Creek Basin, of Rio Blanco Shale Oil Company. (From U.S. Geological Survey.)

uled to run for about four years and to permit a decision on whether or not to enter commercial operations by about 1981. The modified in situ method proposed provides for retorting most of the shale underground. Access will be from vertical shafts, together with sublevel mining methods to prepare the rubblized zone for retorting.

Development on tract C-a started in February 1978 when American Mine Service Company, Contractor, started sinking a 15-foot-diameter shaft to a depth of about 975 feet. A smaller ventilation shaft will be sunk later. Dewatering of the shaft and mining area and construction of surface plant facilities were started prior to shaft sinking. Morrison-Knudsen is the prime contractor for engineering, design and construction.

In March 1979 Rio Blanco Oil Shale Company and Occidental Oil Shale, Inc. entered into a cross-licensing agreement that should result in more rapid use of in situ technology during its earliest development stage. Figure 76 shows the development progress in 1979.

Colorado Lease tract, C-b

This lease tract C-b was obtained February 12, 1974,

under a joint bid by Atlantic Richfield, Ashland Oil, Shell Oil and The Oil Shale Corporation (TOSCO). Atlantic Richfield and TOSCO withdrew from participation in December 1975, and on November 2, 1976, Shell Oil also withdrew. On November 3, 1976, Ashland Petroleum Corporation entered into an agreement with Occidental Oil Shale, Inc. in which the shale would be processed using Occidental's modified in situ technology.

Prior to the Ashland-Occidental joint venture, however, the Detailed Development Plan (DDP) for the tract proposed use of a room-and-pillar mining system with all retorting to be done on the surface. The one-year (1976–77) suspension of operations occurred before this initial DDP was approved. With the entry of Occidental into the program, a new DDP proposing modified in situ development was prepared and was approved in August 1977.

The new DDP proposes to begin operations in a modular fashion so as to permit early evaluation of the modified in situ technology prior to full-scale operations. Test retorts will be operated while development of the commercial mine is underway. Commercial retorts will be developed in groups or clusters with several retorts being operated simultaneously. The oil shale removed during the mining and retorting construction will be disposed of on the surface and possibly surface retorted at a future date. The surface and underground development is aimed at a daily production of 57,000 barrels of shale oil per day by 1985. Three major shafts are being excavated and surface facilities are being erected. This is by far the most massive oil shale development ever attempted on western oil shales. All construction activities are being conducted through contracting, with Ralph M. Parsons Company serving as the managing contractor for all site engineering and construction. Figure 77 shows the rapid progress being made in the development of the C-b lease.

Utah Lease tract, U-a and U-b

Tract U-a was obtained by Phillips Petroleum Company and Sun Oil Company through a joint bid opened March 12, 1974. Tract U-b was awarded to The White River Shale Oil Corporation through bids opened April 9, 1974. The White River Shale Oil Corporation is a joint venture owned by Phillips Petroleum, Sunoco Energy Development Company and SOHIO Natural Resources Company.

The U-a and U-b tracts (Fig 78), during the establishment of the required base-line environmental data, were shown to have naturally occurring background levels of particulates, nonmethane hydrocarbons and ozone occasionally in excess of Federal air standards. The same condition was found on Colorado tracts C-a and C-b. The Utah tracts were granted a one-year suspension of diligence requirements on November 1, 1976. Baseline data continued to be collected, however, and preparation of a Detailed Development Plan continued and was filed on July 1, 1976.

The Detailed Development Plan provided for a modular development approach toward commercialization. The mining method proposed was a room-and-pillar system with access provided through shafts. Retorting was to be all on the surface. The plans provided for controlled expansion following the first or experimental stage to an intermediate stage of 10,000 tons per day, then to a commercial plant producing 100,000 barrels of shale oil per day.

In May 1977, prior to the expiration of the one-year suspension, the lessees of tracts U-a and U-b filed legal actions seeking an injunction to suspend indefinitely the diligence requirements of the lease, including bonus payments, until conflicts with regard to over-

Fig. 77—View of Colorado lease site C-b, Piceance Creek Basin, of Occidental Petroleum Corporation showing shaft towers under construction. (Courtesy of Occidental Petroleum Corporation.)

Fig. 78—View of Utah lease sites U-a, U-b, of the White River Shale Oil Corporation. (From U.S. Geological Survey.)

lapping mining claims, validity of mining claims, and State of Utah rights of selection of the lease area are resolved. The State of Utah has filed claim under provisions of its Statehood Enabling Act of 1894 for right to select the oil shale land in lieu of the sections of land now unavailable because of prior Federal usage. An injunction was granted in June 1977. A 10th Circuit Court of Appeals recently decided against the Federal Government in ruling that Utah is the rightful owner of U-a and U-b, and is entitled to more than $95 million in Federal lease bonus bid payments. The issues associated with overlapping mining claims and the validity of early placer claims is pending. The Court of Appeals decision has been appealed by the U.S. Government.

There is no development work on site at present, and plans for future operations depend upon the resolution of the legal issues. Environmental data continue to be collected.

DEVELOPMENT

Paraho Corporation

Paraho is a contraction of Portuguese words mean-

ing "for the good of mankind." John Jones, a former Bureau of Mines research engineer from the Rifle, Colorado, oil shale facility used this word to describe how he envisioned the results of the application of his patented retort when used to recover oil from the vast western oil shale deposits. In 1973, Jones gathered some 35 companies together in Denver to hear a proposal for demonstrating the effectiveness of his retort on the oil shales of Colorado. The demonstration was to take place at the old Bureau of Mines (now Department of Energy) facility at Anvil Points near Rifle, Colorado, over a three-year period and would require from 7 to 10 million dollars to conduct. After several months of negotiations, 17 companies agreed to participate in and underwrite the demonstration. The participating companies were:

Sohio Petroleum Company	Southern California Edison Co.
Gulf Oil Corporation	The Cleveland-Cliffs Iron Co.
Shell Development Corp.	Atlantic Richfield Co.
Standard Oil Co. (Indiana)	Texaco, Inc.
The Carter Oil Co. (Exxon)	Arthur G. McKee and Co.
Sun Oil Company	Phillips Petroleum Co.
Chevron Research Company	Kerr-McGee Corporation
Marathon Oil Company	Webb-Gray-Chambers-
Mobil Research &	McLorraine Group
Development Corp.	

The Anvil Points plant lying on Naval Oil Shale Reserve property was an ideal location for this research because nearly all of the former facilities were available for use, including the mine. Paraho tested two retorts, one a 30-inch-inside-diameter unit having a nominal capacity of about 20 barrels of oil per day. The second retort was a 126-inch-inside-diameter unit and had about a 200-barrel-per-day capacity (Fig 79). The Bureau's former room-and-pillar mine was reactivated, and some 200,000 tons of oil shale were mined.

The retorts worked well, and field operations that began in 1974 were successfully completed in late 1976. A refinery run of 10,000 barrels of the oil produced was conducted by the U.S. Navy at the Gary Western Refinery at Fruita, Colorado, and the products were tested for military and commercial use. Paraho, during 1976 through 1978, continued to work with the Navy and entered into a contract to provide 100,000 barrels of shale oil so that refinery and product testing for military applications could continue. The Department of Energy provided some funding for this program that was completed late in 1978. The refinery and product testing were continued well into 1979.

The Paraho retort is reported by Harry Pforzheimer, Program Director for Paraho, to have recovered an average of 93 percent of Fisher assay with 89 percent thermal efficiency. All operations conformed to required environmental standards.

The future of the Paraho operation is uncertain as this is written. Jones and Pforzheimer feel that a full-size module (42 feet inside diameter) retort is the next logical step and efforts to provide financing are underway.

Superior Oil Shale Project

The Superior Oil Company owns some 6500 acres of oil shale land on the northern edge of Colorado's Piceance Creek Basin. Exploration and geologic studies were started in 1967 and are continuing. The Superior lands contain nahcolite and dawsonite as well as oil shale. Nahcolite may have an important industrial use in scrubbing sulfur dioxides out of industrial waste gases. Dawsonite can be processed to yield alumina. Considerable research by Superior Oil has been directed toward recovering shale oil, nahcolite and dawsonite. Underground mining with aboveground retorting are planned. However, the Superior Oil land holding consists of long, narrow strips that do not present a favorable configuration for mine development. To obtain a more favorable land position, Superior Oil, in 1973, made formal application to exchange 2572 acres of their land for 1700 acres of adjacent Federal land. The appraisal of mineral values on the lands involved has been completed by the U.S. Geological Survey and a one-year contract for an en-

Fig. 79—View of Paraho Corporation retort installed on Bureau of Mines (now Department of Energy) plant site near Rifle, Colorado. Note oil storage tanks in foreground. (From U.S. Bureau of Mines.)

vironmental impact statement was issued by the Bureau of Land Management in October 1977. The proposed land exchange was denied in February 1980.

Because the Superior Oil Company's property contains dawsonite and nahcolite as well as oil shale, they, in the early 1970s, started development and pilot testing on the recovery of all of these minerals using a retort having a circular grate design.

Their design is similar to the circular grate that is presently operating in La Perla, Mexico to sinter 10,000 tons per day of iron ore pellets at grate temperatures in the range of 2400°F. A pilot unit has been constructed in Cleveland, Ohio and has operated successfully at a throughput of 600 tons per day.

Occidental Petroleum Corporation

The Occidental Petroleum Corporation first began research on in situ methods of obtaining oil from oil shale in 1972. The company was among those that unsuccessfully participated in bidding for oil shale leases in Utah and Colorado in 1974. Occidental obtained the D.A. Shale Oil shale claims in the Logan Wash area northeast of De Beque, Colorado, in 1972 and began extensive research on the modified in situ technology for extraction of shale oil (Fig 80). To date, three small retorts of about 30 feet by 30 feet by 70 feet high have been constructed and operated. Three additional retorts of what may be commercial size (approximately 120–200 feet square by about 300 feet high) have been constructed and operated (Fig 81). These retorts have provided research sites for work on drilling, blasting, fragmentation and methods of construction, as well as research on actual retorting. The oil shale operations of Occidental Petroleum Corporation have been conducted since 1973 by Occidental Oil Shale, Inc.

On September 30, 1977, a cooperative agreement between Occidental and the Department of Energy was signed. This agreement provided for joint Government participation, and funding was made retroactive to November 1, 1976. The overall objectives were for Phase I to provide engineering development work at the Logan Wash site and for Phase II to provide for technical feasibility demonstrations (at the C-b site) of vertical, modified, in situ oil shale retorting processes based upon Occidental designs and prior research and development work. Environmental effects of modified in situ retorting were also to be determined.

On November 2, 1976, Occidental Oil Shale, Inc., joined with Ashland Oil Company in the development of Colorado lease tract C-b. In early 1977, Occidental became the operator of the tract and as of late 1978

held a 75 percent interest in the operations. In February 1979 Ashland withdrew and Occidental became sole operator.

The Phase II section of the agreement between Occidental and the Department of Energy provides for the preparation and operation of a modified in situ demonstration plant with a 2,500-barrel-per-day capacity. In order to achieve this goal and develop commercial potential five shafts are planned, two for the demonstration phase and three additional to provide for commercial operations. The shafts would provide access for underground development of the demonstration and commercial retorts. The commercial retorts would be developed in groups or "clusters" with each such group containing several retorts, all of which would be operated at the same time. The material mined underground and brought to surface during development and retort construction would be stockpiled for possible recovery of contained oil by surface retorts at a later date.

Several tens of thousands of barrels of oil have been produced at Logan Wash, and research will continue at this site during the development of the C-b tract. Work is continuing on both sites.

The Oil Shale Corporation (TOSCO) and Colony Development Operations

Operations of The Oil Shale Corporation, better known as TOSCO, and those of the Colony Development Operations are so closely associated that they are included under this double heading in order to avoid confusion.

All of the early experimental work was contracted to the Denver Research Institute. In 1964, Standard Oil Company of Ohio, The Cleveland-Cliffs Iron Company and TOSCO formed the Colony Development Company. In the same year, Colony Development Company began oil shale operations on land previously owned by Dow Chemical Company near the head of Parachute Creek, about 15 miles north of Grand Valley, Colorado. A pilot plant using the TOSCO II retorting process was constructed, a mine opened and support facilities erected (Fig 82). Operation of a 1000-ton-per-day plant (Fig 83) began in 1965 and continued in 1966 and 1967. In 1969, Atlantic Richfield Company (ARCO) joined Colony and replaced TOSCO as operator. Testing was intensified in 1971 and continued until April 1972. The retort successfully processed more than 1000 tons of oil shale per day, and the mine passed the one-million-ton milestone in total production including research min-

Fig. 80—*Aerial view of Logan Wash operation of Occidental Petroleum Corporation.* (Courtesy of *Occidental Petroleum Corporation.*)

Fig. 81—*Underground view of in situ recovery section of the Logan Wash operation of Occidental Petroleum Corporation.* (Courtesy of *Occidental Petroleum Corporation.*)

Fig. 82—*Aerial view of Colony Development Operations mine and plant on Parachute Creek, north of Grand Valley, Colorado. (From Atlantic Richfield Oil Company.)*

ing. Some 325,000 tons were actually processed and about 270,000 barrels of oil produced. The mine, using a room-and-pillar mining system, is the first to produce a million tons of oil shale in Colorado or from any western oil shale deposit. The shale oil produced also is a record for shale oil production from any one plant processing western oil shales.

In 1973, C. F. Braun and Company was selected as managing contractor for a 45,000-barrel-per-day commercial plant to be constructed at the Parachute location. Environmental studies continued and construction of a road from the Parachute Creek site to the proposed new plant location on the top of the Roan Plateau was started. Design and engineering studies were conducted on both plant and mine. Ashland Oil, Inc. joined the expanded operation in January 1974, and in February 1974 Shell Oil also signed a letter of intent to join. Then, in October 1974, Colony announced that its plans for construction were indefi-

nitely delayed. The reasons given for this action were the very rapid rate of inflation, tight money and the lack of a national energy policy.

By late 1974, Cleveland-Cliffs, SOHIO, Shell Oil and Ashland had terminated their association with Colony Development Operations, leaving only Atlantic Richfield and TOSCO with vested interests.

The suspension of large-scale commercial developments continues into 1979, but Atlantic Richfield and TOSCO have retained their interest, and Colony is continuing to conduct many preconstruction activities but at a reduced pace.

Talley Energy Systems, Incorporated

The Department of Energy and Talley Energy Systems, Inc. entered into an agreement in July 1977 to finance jointly the development and demonstration of a technology for fracturing and retorting shale oil in situ to produce oil from oil shale, with a minimum impact on the environment. The project is designed to evaluate porosity development in an oil shale formation by hydrofracturing, followed by explosive fracturing using Talley Energy's patented liquid explosive.

This in situ test was made at a depth of about 400 feet in the Tipton member of the Green River Formation and is located in Sec. 17, T18N, R106W, Sweetwater County, Wyoming. Evaluation of the explosive fracture system was completed in late 1978. Evaluation of the experiment indicated that the fracturing was not successful and the project was terminated early in 1979.

Geokinetics, Inc.

Geokinetics, Inc., Aminoil USA, Inc. and the Department of Energy entered into an agreement in July 1977 for the purpose of developing, demonstrating and evaluating horizontal in situ retorting technology for use in thin oil shale beds lying near the surface.

Geokinetics has been conducting horizontal retorting research since 1973 and was among those that were unsuccessful in obtaining Government research tracts during the 1974 lease sales.

Fig. 83—View of Colony Development Operations retort, north of Grand Valley, Colorado. (From Atlantic Richfield Oil Company.)

Fig. 84—Shallow horizontal in situ test site of Geokinetics, Inc., south of Vernal, Utah. (1978 photograph by author.)

Fig. 85—Oil recovery equipment on in situ test site of Geokinetics, Inc., south of Vernal, Utah. (1978 photograph by author.)

The project site is the NW¼, Sec 2, T14S, R22E, Uintah County, Utah. This site was being utilized for horizontal retorting research (Fig 84) by Geokinetics prior to the agreement with the Department of Energy. Work under the agreement includes drilling and blasting designed to produce the required porosity for retorting; re-entry drilling for evaluating the blasting technique used and for operational air injection holes, product recovery holes and instrumentation holes; retort preparation including air-flow tests; burning of retort with all retort parameters monitored; and post-retort examination to evaluate the test (Fig 85).

Environmental monitoring is being conducted to include all air parameters and effects on land reclamation.

Geokinetics, Inc. became the largest Utah producer of shale oil in history when some 1700 barrels were produced during 1977. Production in 1978 exceeded that of 1977 and is expected to increase as technology is developed and operations are expanded. In late 1978 or early 1979 Aminoil withdrew its support, and Geokinetics is continuing the research. The company went public on April 30, 1980.

Equity Oil Co., Inc.

Equity Oil Company and the Department of Energy agreed in June 1977 to finance jointly research for the purpose of developing and evaluating true in situ production technology. The project is located on the earlier Equity in situ tract SE¼, Sec. 6, T35, R98W, Black Sulfur Creek, Piceance Creek Basin, Colorado.

This project will continue and extend true in situ research first started by Equity Oil in 1961. During early tests, heated natural gas was injected into the oil shale formation through drill holes and the product was recovered from other drill holes. Some success was reported, but economics apparently did not warrant continuation.

This new research effort will first evaluate the porosity of the leached zone at the test site. If satisfactory, an array of injection wells and recovery wells will be used to inject super-heated steam at high pressure into the formation. Oil will be recovered from the production wells. Technical evaluation of the work will follow. The project is expected to run about two years after steam injection starts.

Laramie Energy Research Center

The Laramie Research Center was started by the U.S. Bureau of Mines for the purpose of conducting research on petroleum and its products. Over the years, the Center became responsible for all phases of oil shale research except mining.

The Laramie Center was among those Bureau Research Centers taken over by the Energy Development Research Agency (ERDA) when it was organized. In turn, ERDA and all of its research centers were absorbed by the Department of Energy when it was formed in 1978.

During past years, the Laramie Research Center has been active in some way in nearly every oil shale venture and has been the Center responsible for the Anvil Points facility as well as for the Naval Oil Shale Reserve in Utah. The history of Laramie Center would require a separate volume to enumerate its many activities. This review will address only the current activities related to research on in situ production of shale oil.

The DOE funded research being conducted by Occidental, Tally-Frac, Equity Oil and Geokinetics are all monitored by the Laramie Center, as is the Paraho operation at Anvil Points. In addition, the Laramie Center has been conducting in situ experiments on the oil shales in the vicinity of Rock Springs, Wyoming, for more than a decade. This work has utilized hydro-fracturing, explosive fracturing and combinations of both at depths up to about 200 feet, followed by retorting in place. The operations have produced some oil, and prospects for increased efficiency have kept the program active. Proposals to increase the scope and magnitude of this work are being made, and it is expected that this research will be continued.

TOSCO Corporation—Sand Wash Project

The early history of The Oil Shale Corporation, which changed its name to the TOSCO Corporation in 1976, was outlined in the section that described the Colony Development Operation.

TOSCO began a solo oil shale effort in Utah in 1976 on about 15,000 acres of State land leases in the Sand Wash area near Vernal. This project proposes a modified in situ operation including surface retorting of the material mined to develop in situ techniques. Preliminary engineering work is under way, and an environment assessment is being conducted on the site. A State of Utah–TOSCO plan requires evaluation of the site to be completed by 1985 and minimum royalty payments to be started in 1984.

TOSCO is directing this project from an office in Vernal and plans to proceed with a test mine if preliminary studies warrant. A full scale development for a commercial operation would require about 4 years.

Early in 1979, TOSCO obtained permits from the State of Utah to sink a 12-foot diameter shaft to a depth of 2400 feet on its Sand Wash property. Initial field work was scheduled to begin in 1979 and was expected to require from two to three years to complete.

Union Oil Co., Inc.

The early history of the Union Oil Company's activities in oil shale was reviewed previously in discussing its land acquisitions of the 1920s and its operation of a mine and retort on its Parachute Creek holdings in the 1950s.

Union Oil has conducted research and studied shale oil economics since the 1920s and continues to do so. In

early 1974, the company announced that it was planning a commercial operation of from 50,000 barrels per day to as much as 150,000 barrels per day on its private shale lands near Grand Valley, Colorado. This construction was dependent upon favorable economic conditions and elimination of any major environmental obstacles. Apparently, the criteria have not been met because there has been no such construction.

In early 1978, Union Oil revealed plans for construction of an experimental plant using a commercial-size retort with some $128 million of its own funds. Again, this investment was contingent upon an investment and regulatory climate meeting Union's needs. This project would process some 10,000 tons of shale, obtained from room-and-pillar mining, in a retort of Union Oil's design that would produce about 7,000

Fig. 86—*View of rig used to drill 10-foot diameter shaft to a depth of 2370 feet. U.S. Bureau of Mines project, Piceance Creek, Colorado. (From U.S. Bureau of Mines.)*

Fig. 87—*Placing of 8-foot diameter casing in Bureau of Mines drilled shaft. Piceance Creek Basin, Colorado. (From U.S. Bureau of Mines.)*

barrels of oil per day. Again, conditions have not warranted Union Oil proceeding, and this prototype facility has not been started. Union Oil has proposed that the Department of Energy provide financing on a cost-sharing basis. This proposal is still pending.

U.S. Bureau of Mines

In 1976, the Bureau of Mines and the Bureau of Land Management entered into an agreement to: (1) develop a research facility for use by the Bureau of Mines in testing, developing and demonstrating new or improved underground methods of mining oil shale and associated minerals, and extracting shale oil by modified in situ methods, and (2) obtaining and making available to the Bureau of Land Management information on geology, hydrology, mineral resources and mining methods. In addition to research on the environmental aspects of oil shale mining, initial Bureau plans called for development of a prototype demonstration mine to facilitate full-scale testing, evaluation and demonstration of several promising underground mining methods.

A site was selected in Horsedraw, a tributary of Piceance Creek, and an Environmental Analysis Report of the site was completed by the Bureau of Land Management in April 1976.

During the calendar year 1977, a Bureau contractor blind-bored a 120-inch diameter shaft to a total depth of 2,371 feet and installed 96-inch-inside-diameter steel casing to a depth of 2,352 feet (Fig 86 and Fig 87). Cementing of the casing was completed in December 1977. The lower 1600 feet of the shaft penetrates virtually the full thickness of oil shale and accessory saline minerals in the Parachute Creek member of the Green River Formation underlying the research tract.

The shaft has been equipped for mining, and some bulk samples of the dawsonite oil shale and nahcolite have been obtained.

Multi Mineral Corporation of Houston, Texas, entered into a cooperative agreement with the Bureau of Mines in late April 1979 and it is expected research will be continued on this site.

PART V

SUMMARY AND EPILOGUE

Summary

It has long been recognized that oil shale has the potential of augmenting our conventional petroleum supplies. However, for a variety of reasons, the use of this vast resource has not been developed although attempts to do so have taken place at various times for over 60 years. Research on western oil shale might be said to have started when Robert Catlin began his Elko, Nevada, work in 1915. During the next 15 years there was considerable activity involving western oil shales. Oil shale claims were located, and a few small recovery plants were erected in Colorado, Nevada, Utah, Wyoming and Montana. A little shale oil was produced. However, the major oil companies were not interested in producing shale oil and the small operator did not have the needed capital or the technical knowhow. This early boom saw less than 15 plants produce a total of less than 15,000 barrels of shale oil and of this total all but about 500 barrels was produced by the Catlin Operation in Nevada and by the U.S. Bureau of Mines Rulison, Colorado, operation. Increased supplies of natural petroleum and its lower price resulted in the termination of all western oil shale development efforts by 1930.

The period from 1930 to about 1944 was one of plentiful petroleum supplies at reasonable prices. Oil shale development was at its lowest ebb.

Shortages of petroleum during World War II caused a resurgence of interest in oil shale. The period from 1940 to 1969 saw the first large-scale mining and retorting operations in oil shale, and the first attempts at true in situ recovery of the shale oil. Approximately 75,000 barrels of shale oil were produced, but the major advancements were in developing mine designs and technology, and in retort design and technology.

Activities from 1969 to 1973 were, at best, slow.

Attempts by the U.S. Government to lease oil shale lands failed. The most active company was the Colony Development Operation, Colorado, that continued research and operation of a 1000-ton-per-day plant started in the mid-1960s. Over 250,000 barrels of shale oil were produced and over one million tons of shale were mined.

The oil embargo of 1973 together with a new offering of oil shale leases by the Government in 1974 resulted in the most concentrated efforts for shale oil production to date. Occidental Oil Shale, Inc. began a modified in situ research program on private land in Colorado and became partner in and then sole operator of the Colorado C-b Lease tract. Occidental is now developing this tract for commercial production. Rio Blanco Oil Shale Company is developing a modified in situ research facility on Colorado Lease tract C-a. This will be expanded for commercial production if the research efforts are successful. Paraho constructed a surface retort on the old Bureau of Mines Rifle, Colorado, facility and produced over 100,000 barrels of oil for the U.S. Navy. The Utah Lease tracts became inactive pending settlement of land ownership disputes, but plan to resume work when ownership is settled. Geokinetics became the first to market shale oil in Utah from their operation of a near-surface, true in situ, research project.

It is estimated that the total production of shale oil from 1915 through 1978 has been in excess of 500,000 barrels. Most of this has been produced in Colorado.

The continuing shortage of United States and world petroleum together with the economics of production will determine whether this current effort to produce shale oil is more successful than those efforts of the past.

Epilogue

NOTE, BY THE AUTHOR

I began this dissertation with a 1922 statement regarding the fear of an inadequate oil supply. It seems appropriate to end it with an even older but equally appropriate quotation.

> "The day that some company undertaking the production of oil through the distillation of oil shales in this country proves, through actual practice, that oil may be produced successfully and continuously on a commercial scale at its plant, a new page will be turned in the industrial history of the United States. The significance of the first genuine production at a profit is hardly likely to be overestimated."

The above paragraph is from a letter written by George Otis, Director, U.S. Geological Survey, December 19, 1918.

NOTE, BY THE EDITOR,
Arnold H. Pelofsky

Oil shale has had a checkered past. In the early 1920s, again in the late 40s and early 50s, oil shale became a prominent energy resource. But, alas, oil shale was not exploited during these periods. In the 1920s oil shale was not exploited because of the substantial finds of oil in Texas and then in Oklahoma. In the 1950s, oil shale was again reduced to a curiosity because of the substantial oil finds in Arabia.

Now we are again in a similar situation, due primarily to our reliance on energy from foreign sources and its cost, where oil shale is once more being considered as a secure indigenous energy source.

Its location is known; we do not have to hunt for it. The organic matter, kerogen, in the shale has essentially the same carbon-hydrogen ratio as conventional crude oil. As the text of this book suggests, merely heating the rock (retorting) is all that is required to produce a product that can be further refined to usable products using present-day technology. There are some who even suggest that the shale oil produced from the retort can be used "as is" as an acceptable boiler fuel. Others wish to refine it to aviation grade fuels and to diesel oils. There is no one acceptable solution. Each producer, given his own particular market, will have to make this decision. This book describes the many retorting processes that have been proposed to extract the kerogen from the oil shale located in the western United States. There are many reasons why the exploitation of oil shale has never progressed further; these are political, technical, environmental, and economic.

The United States Government owns 80 percent of the resources which can be found in 1,500 square miles located primarily in the States of Colorado, Utah and Wyoming. In this area, it is claimed that there are about two trillion barrels of oil trapped in the marstone we call oil shale. Scientists and engineers believe that 640 million barrels are recoverable using present-day retorting technology.

The Federal Government wants to be absolutely certain that the people of the United States are protected. The Government does not want to be accused of a "land giveaway". It does not want another "Tea Pot Dome" scandal. As a result, oil shale land is not leased on a continual basis, and land claims are still being challenged by Governmental agencies in the courts.

In order for a company or companies to become seriously involved, however, they must have sufficient resource to ensure that they can successfully feed an oil shale complex with oil shale for an extended period of time. They will want to be able to expand capacity either by constructing additional plants or by enlarging existing ones. If the Government will not lease or sell the land on an "as needed" basis, the risk of having to close down a multi-million dollar complex after only twenty or thirty years of operation is unacceptably high.

At least two books have been written that explain the political history quite thoroughly. They are *The Rock that Burns* by Harry K. Savage* and *Elusive Bonanza* by Christopher Welles†. Even though these books were written some time ago, they are still relevant. Paul Russell's book includes descriptions of retorting technology from before 1900 to the present, but the retorts described are essentially pilot-plant size. If any of those retorts were scaled up to commercial size and tested, the United States—even the world—would be further along in reducing the technological risk. Only after a commercially sized retort is operating in a commercial facility can actual operating data be accumulated. Such data are needed to assess the problems, to attempt to solve them and, by so doing, to improve the process.

Even though the retort is the heart of a facility used to recover a usable product from oil shale, it represents only 15–20 percent of the overall capital investment. Mining represents 50 percent, and mining technology still leaves a lot to be desired. When it comes to underground mining, especially in gassy mines, mining equipment capable of removing large tonnages of material in the neighborhood of 100,000–200,000 tons per day is still lacking. We have a vicious cycle. Do we start hauling these large tonnages and then develop more sophisticated equipment or do we first develop the equipment and then mine and haul all of the rock? In the latter case, the mining equipment manufacturers are reluctant to assume the risk of developing expensive equipment without the certainty of selling it to someone. As a result, they are waiting for an industry before they get involved, while industry is waiting on them.

The environmental laws of the land require that the oil shale complex is not harmful to the ecostructure of the region. Many environmental impact statements have been written about the environmental effects on the land, the air and the water, as well as on living things. Although these laws may be needed, they have delayed the start of an oil shale industry. At the time of this note some projects have been delayed for over five years because of potentially harmful environmental effects. What makes the situation untenable to some is that we really do not know, with certainty, what will be the actual effects of a commercial complex on the environment. Yet, if a facility is constructed and allowed to operate, then it may be too late to protect the environment. Of course, the facility could be shut down, but this premise creates an undue risk for those companies interested in constructing and operating such a plant. Again a vicious cycle.

All of the above issues affect economics. An oil shale industry is required, if for no other reason than that it would provide national security. How long can the United States rely on foreign sources of oil? For approximately every $10,000.00 that leave the United States, there is one less job in the United States. When we evaluate the economics of a shale oil industry, we compare the price of the product derived from shale with that of the product derived from conventional crude oil. Since the price of foreign crude oil is arbitrarily set, the price of the product derived from it is also arbitrary. The foreign sellers of crude oil can always lower the price of their commodity so as to be lower than the price of shale oil. If this happens, it is difficult for shale oil to compete. This risk affects the ability of companies to gain financing because very few of them have the necessary collateral to satisfy the banking community, especially since the technology has not been commercially proven, resource ownership is increasingly in question, and environmental effects are in doubt.

All of the above translates to the need for subsidy to those companies interested in constructing and operating a commercial oil shale facility. These subsidies could take the form of loan guarantees, price support, and/or outright purchase of the product at a specified price. At this moment in time, the Federal and pertinent State Governments are intensively studying the above issues. Hopefully, in the not too distant future, we will be able to say, "Yes, Virginia, there really is an oil shale industry".

---

*1967. Boulder, Colorado: Pruett Press.
†1970. New York: Dutton.

References

1. Gavin, M.J. 1922. Oil Shale, An Historical, Technical and Economic Study. *Bulletin 210, U.S.* Bureau of mines.
2. Ibid., p. 9.
3. McKee, Ralph H. 1925. *Shale Oil* (New York: Reinhold), p. 14.
4. Winchester, Dean E. 1923. Oil Shale of the Rocky Mountain Region. *Bulletin 729,* U.S. Geological Survey.
5. Gavin, M. J. 1922. Oil Shale, An Historical, Technical and Economic Study. *Bulletin 210,* pp. 10–17, U.S. Bureau of Mines.
6. Alderson, V. C. 1920. *The Oil Shale Industry* (New York: F. A. Stokes), p. 5.
7. Gavin. M. J. 1922. Oil Shale, An Historical, Technical and Economic Study. *Bulletin 210,* p. 99, U.S. Bureau of Mines.
8. Lewis, W. R. 1920. Seeing the Oil Fields. *The Mountain States Mineral Age,* vol. 5, no. 6, Sept., pp. 17–32.
9. Alderson, V. C. 1920. *The Oil Shale Industry* (New York: F. A. Stokes), p. 35.
10. Lewis, W. R. 1920. Seeing the Oil Fields. *The Mountain States Mineral Age,* vol. 5, no. 6, Sept., pp. 17–32.
11. Gavin, M. J. 1922. Oil Shale, An Historical, Technical and Economic Study. *Bulletin 210,* pp. 99, 100, U.S. Bureau of Mines.
12. Lewis, W. R. 1920. Seeing the Oil Fields. *The Mountain States Mineral Age,* vol. 5, no. 6, Sept., pp. 17–32.
13. Records. 1930. U.S. General Land Office, Department of the Interior, Denver, Colorado.
14. Article. 1923. *The Railroad Red Book,* vol. 40, no. 1, Jan., p. 14.
15. Gavin, M. J. 1922. Oil Shale, An Historical, Technical and Economic Study. *Bulletin 210,* pp. 99, 100, U.S. Bureau of Mines.
16. Article. 1920. *The Railroad Red Book,* vol. 27, no. 1, Jan., p. 21.
17. Article. 1919. *The Engineering and Mining Journal,* vol. 105, no. 5, Dec., pp. 218–219.
18. Article 1920. *Engineering and Mining Journal-Press,* vol. 114, no. 16, July, p. 816.
19. Wadleigh, F. A. 1922. Article in *The Railroad Red Book,* vol. 39, no. 1, Jan., p. 71.
20. Letter. 1919. *Wadleigh Collection,* Dec., Colorado Historical Society, Denver, Colorado.
21. Article. 1922. Placer Machine Recovers Free Gold from Oil Shale Deposits. *The Shale Review,* vol. 4, no. 9, Sept., p. 6.
22. McGee, R. E. 1920. Article in *The Searchlight Oil Shale Industry,* Mar., p. 1.
23. Alderson, V. C. 1922. Oil Shale–a Resumé for 1921. *The Railroad Red Book,* vol. 39, no. 1, Jan., pp. 7–14.
24. Gavin, M. J. 1922. Oil Shale, An Historical, Technical and Economic Study. *Bulletin 210,* pp. 101–103, U.S. Bureau of Mines.
25. Ibid., p. 108.
26. McKee, Ralph H. 1925. *Shale Oil* (New York: Reinhold), pp. 152–169.
27. Ibid., p. 60.
28. Redwood, A. B. 1913. *Treatsie [sic] on Petroleum.* London, England.
29. Mineral Resources. 1921. Department of the Interior, Washington, D.C.
30. Letter. 1923. *Wadleigh Collection,* Colorado Historical Society, Denver, Colorado.
31. Mineral Resources. 1927. Department of the Interior, Washington, D.C.
32. Report. 1921. Colorado Bureau of Mines, Denver, Colorado.
33. Jones, C. L. 1920. Activity in the Development of the Rocky Mountain Oil Shale Region. *Mellon Institute Report,* Oct.
34. Prospectus. 1920. Oil Shale Mining Co. Solicitors Office, Department of the Interior, Denver, Colorado.
35. Article. 1918. *The Denver Post,* Apr. 7, Denver, Colorado.
36. McGee, R. E. 1920. Article in *The Searchlight Oil Shale Industry,* Mar., p. 1.
37. Report. 1930. Inspectors Report, General Land Office, Department of the Interior, Denver, Colorado.
38. Article. 1919. *The Shale Review,* vol. 1, no. 6, July, p. 3.
39. Article. 1920. *The Shale Review,* vol. 2, no. 2, Mar.
40. Article. 1920. *The Shale Review,* vol. 2, no. 1, Jan.–Feb., p. 3.
41. Letter. 1920. *Wadleigh Collection,* Colorado Historical Society, Denver, Colorado.
42. Article. 1920. *The Shale Review,* vol. 2, no. 1, Jan.–Feb., p. 4.
43. Gavin, M. J., and Desmond, J. S. 1930. Construction and Operation of the Bureau of Mines Experimental Oil-Shale Plant, 1925–27. *Bulletin 315,* U.S. Bureau of Mines.
44. Ibid., pp. 5–7.
45. Ibid., p. 18.
46. Ibid., pp. 18–20.

47. Letter. 1922. Town of De Beque, Solicitors Office, Department of the Interior, Denver Colorado.
48. Letter. 1922. *Wadleigh Collection,* Colorado Historical Society, Denver, Colorado.
49. Ibid.
50. Alderson, V. C. 1920. *The Oil Shale Industry* (New York: F. A. Stokes), p. 6.
51. Article. 1925. The Colorado Oil Shale Industry. *Mining Congress Journal,* Aug., p. 404.
52. Alderson, V. C. 1920. The Present Status of the Oil Shale Industry. *The Railroad Red Book,* vol. 37, no. 1, Jan., pp. 19–31.
53. McKee, Ralph H. 1925. *Shale Oil* (New York: Reinhold), p. 164.
54. Report. 1921. Colorado Carbon Co. to the Colorado Bureau of Mines, Denver, Colorado.
55. Report. 1923. Hearing Examiners Report, Mar. 2, General Land Office, Department of the Interior, Denver, Colorado.
56. Ibid.
57. Deed. 1955. Page 452, Reception no. 190902, Book 286, Aug. 13, Garfield County, Colorado.
58. Report. 1927. Hearings, General Land Office, Department of the Interior, Denver, Colorado.
59. McKee, Ralph H. 1925. *Shale Oil* (New York: Reinhold), p. 153.
60. Files. 1922. General Land Office, Department of the Interior, Denver, Colorado.
61. Article. 1921. *The Shale Review,* vol. 3, no. 7, Aug.-Sept., p. 6.
62. Files. 1968. Solicitors Office, Department of the Interior, Denver, Colorado.
63. Article. 1921. *The Shale Review,* vol. 3, no. 10, Dec., p. 18.
64. Article. 1922. *The Shale Review,* vol. 4, no. 2, Feb.-Mar., p. 6.
65. Company reports. 1921–1927. Index Oil Shale Co. to the Colorado Bureau of Mines, Denver, Colorado.
66. Articles of receivership. 1928. Index Oil Shale Co., Sept. 6, Garfield County, Colorado.
67. Article. 1922. *The Shale Review,* vol. 4, no. 2, Feb. Mar.
68. Article. 1922. *The Shale Review,* vol. 4, no. 3, Apr., p. 12.
69. Letter. 1922. *Wadleigh Collection,* Colorado Historical Society, Denver, Colorado.
70. Article. 1924. A Colorado Oil Shale Development. *Chemical and Metallurgical Engineering,* vol. 31, no. 20, Nov. 17, pp. 773–775.
71. Complaint (Lien). 1928. District Court, July 28, Garfield County, Colorado.
72. Ibid.
73. Ibid.
74. Ibid.
75. Freeman, J. D. 1964. *Rocky Mountain Oil Reporter,* Feb., pp. 6–8.
76. Report. 1920. Mineral Examiners Report, Nov. 20, General Land Office, Department of the Interior, Denver, Colorado.
77. Ibid.
78. Ibid.
79. Article. 1921. *The Railroad Red Book,* vol. 38, no. 1, Jan., p. 9.
80. Article. 1922. *The Railroad Red Book,* vol. 39, no. 11, Nov., p. 11.
81. Report. 1922. Inspectors Report, Colorado Bureau of Mines, Denver, Colorado.
82. Depositions. 1968. Solicitors Office, Department of the Interior, Denver, Colorado.
83. Incorporation records. 1933. State of Colorado.
84. Report. 1921. The Monarch Oil Shale Co. to Colorado Bureau of Mines, Denver, Colorado.
85. Letter. 1920. *Wadleigh Collection,* Colorado Historical Society, Denver, Colorado.
86. Article. 1920. *The Shale Review,* vol. 2, no. 4, May.
87. Alderson, V. C. 1921. Oil Shale Activity. *Circular of Information,* Aug., Colorado School of Mines, Golden, Colorado.
88. Jones. C. L. 1920. Activity in the Development of the Rocky Mountain Oil Shale Region. *Mellon Institute Report,* Oct., p. 49.
89. Letter. 1922. *Wadleigh Collection,* Colorado Historical Society, Denver, Colorado.
90. Article. 1922. *The Shale Review,* vol. 4, no. 2, Feb., p. 4.
91. Letter. 1928. Secretary of State, Colorado, to Inspector, General Land Office, Department of the Interior, Denver, Colorado, Apr. 20.
92. Report. 1928. Inspectors Report, Colorado Bureau of Mines, Denver, Colorado.
93. Letter. 1921. *Wadleigh Collection,* Colorado Historical Society, Denver, Colorado.
94. Article. 1919. *The Shale Review,* vol. 1, no. 6., p. 21.
95. Article. 1919. *The Shale Review,* vol. 1, no. 3, p. 9.
96. Marsh, C. B. 1920. Oil Shale—The New Industry. *Oil and Gas News,* June.
97. Advertising Circular. 1920. Issued by Mount Logan Oil Shale & Refining Co.
98. Winchester, Dean E. 1921. Addition to *Bulletin 729,* U.S. Geological Survey.
99. Alderson, V. C. 1922. Oil Shale—A Resumé for 1921. *The Railroad Red Book,* vol. 39, no. 1, pp. 7–14.
100. Report. 1919. Inspectors Report, July 12, Colorado Bureau of Mines, Denver, Colorado.
101. Report. 1922. Inspectors Report, Colorado Bureau of Mines, Denver, Colorado.
102. Letter. 1920. *Wadleigh Collection.* Colorado Historical Society, Denver, Colorado.
103. Article. 1921. *The Shale Review,* vol. 3, no. 4, May, p. 11.
104. Article. 1921. *The Shale Review,* vol. 3, no. 3, Mar., p. 5.
105. Letter. 1922. Solicitors Office, Jan., Department of the Interior, Denver, Colorado.
106. Circular. 1920. Issued by Mount Logan Oil Shale & Refining Co., and
     Report. 1930. Inspectors Report, Feb. 28. General Land Office, Department of the Interior, Denver, Colorado.
107. Letter. 1920. *Wadleigh Collection,* Dec. 18, Colorado Historical Society, Denver, Colorado.

108. Report. 1930. Inspectors Report, Feb. 18, General Land Office, Department of the Interior, Denver, Colorado.
109. Records Contest 12279. 1930. General Land Office, Department of the Interior, Denver, Colorado.
110. Incorporation records. 1930. The Oil Shale Mining Co., Feb. 18., State of Colorado.
111. Ibid.
112. Report. 1917. The Oil Shale Mining Co., May 7, to Colorado Bureau of Mines, Denver, Colorado.
113. Report. 1930. Inspectors Report, Jan. 31, General Land Office, Department of the Interior, Denver, Colorado.
114. Ibid.
115. Gavin, M. J. 1922. Oil Shale, An Historical, Technical and Economic Study. *Bulletin 210,* p. 102, U. S. Bureau of Mines.
116. Winchester, Dean E. 1923. Oil Shale of the Rocky Mountain Region. *Bulletin 729,* U.S. Geological Survey.
117. Report. 1930. Inspectors Report, Jan., General Land Office, Department of the Interior, Denver, Colorado.
118. Ibid.
119. Article. 1919. *The Shale Review,* vol. 1, no. 12, Dec., p. 18.
120. Article. 1920. *The Shale Review,* vol. 2, no. 6, Aug.
121. Jones, C. L. 1920. Activity in the Development of the Rocky Mountain Oil Shale Region. *Mellon Institute Report,* Oct.
122. Telegram. 1921. *Wadleigh Collection,* May 21, Colorado Historical Society, Denver, Colorado.
123. Report. 1921. The Oil Shale Mining Co. to the Colorado Bureau of Mines, Denver, Colorado.
124. Article. 1919. *The Shale Review,* vol. 1, no. 11, Nov.
125. Article. 1920. *The Shale Review,* vol. 2, no. 4, July, p. 14.
126. Prospectus. 1920. The Oil Shale Mining Co. [this book].
127. Report. 1930. Inspectors Report, Jan., General Land Office, Department of the Interior, Denver, Colorado.
128. Report. 1917. The Oil Shale Mining Co., Dec., to Colorado Bureau of Mines, Denver, Colorado.
129. Report. 1925. The Oil Shale Mining Co. to the Colorado Bureau of Mines, Denver, Colorado.
130. Reports. 1922, 1923, 1924. The Oil Shale Mining Co. to Colorado Bureau of Mines, Denver, Colorado, May 1, Apr. 30 and May 1.
131. Report. 1925. The Oil Shale Mining Co. to Colorado Bureau of Mines, Denver, Colorado.
132. Report. 1930. Inspectors Report, Jan., General Land Office, Department of the Interior, Denver, Colorado.
133. Report. 1926. The Oil Shale Mining Co., July, to Colorado Bureau of Mines, Denver, Colorado.
134. Report. 1930. Inspectors Report, Jan., General Land Office, Department of the Interior, Denver, Colorado.
135. Incorporation records. 1930. State of Colorado.

136. Report. 1930. Inspectors Report, Jan., General Land Office, Department of the Interior, Denver, Colorado.
137. Ibid., p. 49.
138. Koepoke, Henry. 1919. Audit of Searchlight Oil and Mining Co., Dec. 19, Denver, Colorado.
139. Article. 1922. *The Shale Review,* vol. 4, no. 2, Feb., p. 10.
140. Murry, D. Keith (ed.) 1974. *Guidebook to the Energy Resources of the Piceance Creek Basin, Colorado* (Denver, Colorado: Rocky Mountain Association of Geologists), p. 145.
141. Article. 1920. *Mountain States Mineral Age,* vol. 5, no. 6, p. 21.
142. Alderson, V. C. 1921. Oil Shale Activity. *Circular of Information,* Aug., Colorado School of Mines, Golden, Colorado.
143. Winchester, Dean E. 1923. Oil Shale of the Rocky Mountain Region. *Bulletin 729,* U.S. Geological Survey.
144. Report. 1928. Ventura-Colorado Oil Company to Texas Co., Apr. 20.
145. Ibid.
146. Article. 1922. *The Railroad Red Book,* vol. 40, no. 1, Jan.
147. Article. 1923. *The Railroad Red Book,* vol. 41, no. 1, p. 14.
148. Article. 1921. *The Mountain States Mineral Age,* vol. 6, no. 4, p. 20.
149. Report. 1923. Inspectors Report, Jan., Colorado Bureau of Mines, Denver, Colorado.
150. New Oil Shale Plant in Construction near De Beque. 1925. Article in *The Mountain States Mineral Age,* vol. 10, no. 1, Nov., p. 13.
151. Report. 1925. *The Mountain States Mineral Age,* vol. 10, no. 2, p. 21.
152. Report. 1926. Inspectors Report, June 20, Colorado Bureau of Mines.
153. Article. 1926. *The Mountain States Mineral Age,* vol. 11, no. 11, Nov.
154. Article. 1927. *The Mountain States Mineral Age,* vol. 12, no. 2, Feb., p. 9.
155. Report. 1927. Inspectors Report, Nov. 10, Colorado Bureau of Mines, Denver, Colorado.
156. Report. 1929. Washington Shale Oil and Products Co., Mar. 3, to State of Colorado.
157. Department of the Interior. 1927. Mineral Resources. Department of the Interior, Washington, D.C.
158. Report. 1929. Washington Shale Oil and Products Co., Mar. 3, to State of Colorado.
159. Memorandum. 1966. Secretary of State of Washington, Oct. 21, to Bureau of Land Management, Department of the Interior, Denver, Colorado.
160. Winchester, Dean E. 1923. Memorandum to the Press, Apr. 26, Department of the Interior.
161. Alderson, V. C. 1920. *The Oil Shale Industry* (New York: F. A. Stokes).
162. McKee, Ralph H. 1925. *Shale Oil* (New York: Reinhold), p. 165.

163. Colorado Contest 356 and 360. 1968. Bureau of Land Management, Department of the Interior, Denver, Colorado.

164. Catlin, R. M. 1875. Pencil notes. Solicitors Office, Department of the Interior, Denver, Colorado.

165. Catlin, R. M. *Who Was Who In North America, 1897-1942.*

166. Files. 1918. Quit Claim Deed, Mar. Solicitors Office, Department of the Interior, Denver, Colorado.

167. Catlin, R. M. 1875. Pencil notes. Solicitors Office, Department of the Interior, Denver, Colorado.

168. Ibid.

169. Files. 1916. Lease no. 4349F, Central Pacific Railroad. Solicitors Office, Department of the Interior, Denver, Colorado.

170. Catlin, R. M. 1916. Letter to Central Pacific Railroad. Solicitors Office, Department of the Interior, Denver, Colorado.

171. Ibid.

172. Mull, J. B. 1968. Direct Testimony, Colorado Contest 360. Solicitors Office, Department of the Interior, Denver, Colorado.

173. Catlin, R. M. 1918. Income Tax Return. Solicitors Office, Department of the Interior, Denver, Colorado.

174. Catlin, R. M. 1918. Quit Claim Deed. Solicitors Office, Department of the Interior, Denver, Colorado.

175. Winchester, Dean E. 1923. Oil Shale of the Rocky Mountain Region. *Bulletin 729,* U.S. Geological Survey.

176. Wadleigh, F. A. 1919. Oil Shale Notes Salt Lake and Elko Trip, Mar. 25-29. *Wadleigh Collection,* Colorado Historical Society, Denver, Colorado.

177. Mull, J. B. 1968. Direct Testimony, Colorado Contest 360. Solicitors Office, Department of the Interior, Denver, Colorado.

178. Sheeler, W. L. 1920. Mining at the Catlin Property. *The Mountain States Mineral Age,* vol. 5, no. 6, Sept.

179. Reports. 1922, 1923, 1924. Catlin Shale Products Co. to Nevada State Mine Inspector, June 26, June 13 and May 17.

180. Reports. 1918-1929. Catlin Shale Products Co. to Nevada State Mine Inspector.

181. Wadleigh, F. A. 1919. Oil Shale Notes Salt Lake and Elko Trip, Mar. 25-29. *Wadleigh Collection,* Colorado Historical Society, Denver, Colorado.

182. Sheeler, W. L. 1919. Letter, Oct. 13. *Wadleigh Collection,* Colorado Historical Society, Denver, Colorado.

183. Catlin, R. M. 1919. Letter, Aug. 6. *Wadleigh Collection,* Colorado Historical Society, Denver, Colorado.

184. Mull, J. B. 1968. Direct Testimony, Colorado Contest 360. Solicitors Office, Department of the Interior, Denver, Colorado.

185. Ibid.

186. Ibid.

187. Ibid.

188. Sheeler, W. L. 1924. Letter, Oct. 27. *Wadleigh Collection,* Colorado Historical Society, Denver, Colorado.

189. Reports. 1919-1924. Catlin Shale Products Co. to Nevada State Mine Inspector.

190. Catlin, R. M. 1922. Letter to David Day, Oct. 24. Solicitors Office, Department of the Interior, Denver, Colorado.

191. Mull, J. B. 1968. Direct Testimony, Colorado Contest 360. Solicitors Office, Department of the Interior, Denver, Colorado.

192. Letter. 1924. Consolidated Copper Company (Nevada), July 12, to Catlin Shale Products Co. Solicitors Office, Department of the Interior, Denver, Colorado.

193. Letter. 1924. Ruhm, H. D. (Chemicals) to R. M. Catlin, Jan. 25. Solicitors Office, Department of the Interior, Denver, Colorado.

194. Mull, J. B. 1968. Direct Testimony, Colorado Contest 360. Solicitors Office, Department of the Interior, Denver, Colorado.

195. Ibid.

196. Ibid.

197. Ibid.

198. Letter. 1924. Secretary of Navy Wilbur, May 31, to H. D. Ruhm. Solicitors Office, Department of the Interior, Denver, Colorado.

199. Letters. 1924. H. D. Ruhm, Feb. 18 and Mar. 28, to R. M. Catlin. Solicitors Office, Department of the Interior, Denver, Colorado.

200. Letter. 1924. H. D. Ruhm, May 22, to Thomas D. Jones. Solicitors Office, Department of the Interior, Denver, Colorado.

201. Mull, J. B. 1968. Direct Testimony, Colorado Contest 360. Solicitors Office, Department of the Interior, Denver, Colorado.

202. Report. 1925. Catlin Shale Products Co., May 23, to Nevada State Mine Inspector.

203. Mull, J. B. 1968. Direct Testimony, Colorado Contest 360. Solicitors Office, Department of the Interior, Denver, Colorado.

204. Ibid.

205. Ibid.

206. Jones, C. L. 1920. Activity in the Development of the Rocky Mountain Oil Shale Region. *Mellon Institute Report,* Oct., p. 68.

207. Winchester, Dean E. 1923. Oil Shale of the Rocky Mountain Region. Memorandum for the Press, Apr. 26., Department of the Interior, Denver, Colorado.

208. Gavin, M. J. 1922. Oil Shale, An Historical, Technical and Economic Study. *Bulletin 210,* U.S. Bureau of Mines, p. 103.

209. Alderson, V. C. 1920. *The Oil Shale Industry* (New York: F. A. Stokes), p. 212.

210. Jones, C. L. 1920. Activity in the Development of the Rocky Mountain Oil Shale Region. *Mellon Institute Report,* Oct., p. 68.

211. Jones, J. B. 1919. Letter. *Wadleigh Collection,* Colorado Historical Society, Denver, Colorado.

212. Wood, H. L. 1920. *National Petroleum News,* vol. 2, no. 9, Sept., p. 9.

213. McKee, Ralph H. 1925. *Shale Oil* (New York: Reinhold), p. 164.

214. Crawford, Arthur L. 1961. Oil Shale on Chris's Creek, Juab County, Utah. *Circular 41,* Utah Geological and Mineralogical Survey, Salt Lake City, Utah.

215. Winchester, Dean E. 1916. Oil Shale of the Uinta Basin, Northeastern Utah. *Bulletin 691,* U.S. Geological Survey.

216. Article. 1919. *Engineering and Mining Journal,* vol. 107, no. 5, Feb., pp. 218–219.

217. Wood, H: L. 1920. *National Petroleum News,* vol. 2, no. 9, Sept., p. 9.

218. Jones, C. L. 1920. Activity in the Development of the Rocky Mountain Oil Shale Region. *Mellon Institute Report,* Oct., pp. 53, 75.

219. Alderson, V. C. 1922. Oil Shale—a Resumé for 1921. *The Railroad Red Book,* vol. 39, no. 1, Jan., pp. 7–14.

220. Wood. H. L. 1920. *National Petroleum News,* vol. 2, no. 9, Sept.

221. Winchester, Dean E. 1921. Addition to *Bulletin 729,* U.S. Geological Survey.

222. Article. 1922. *The Railroad Red Book,* vol. 39, no. 1, Jan., p. 9.

223. Ibid, p. 13.

224. Winchester, Dean E. 1923. Oil Shale of the Rocky Mountain Region, Memorandum for the Press, Apr. 26. Department of the Interior, Denver, Colorado.

225. Alderson, V. C. 1922. Oil Shale—a Resumé for 1921. *The Railroad Red Book,* vol. 39, no. 1, Jan., pp. 7–14.

226. Alderson, V. C. 1927. Oil Shale Progress. *Mining Congress Journal,* Dec., p. 885.

227. Articles of Incorporation. 1929. State of Wyoming. Wyoming Historical Society.

228. Jones, C. L. 1920. Activity in the Development of the Rocky Mountain Oil Shale Region. *Mellon Institute Report,* Oct., pp. 43, 90.

229. East, J. H., and Gardner, E. D. 1964. Oil Shale Mining, Rifle, Colorado, 1944–1956. *Bulletin 611,* U.S. Bureau of Mines.

230. Oil Shale Demonstration Plant, Rifle, Colorado. 1952. Brochure. U.S. Bureau of Mines.

231. Staff. 1974. Program for In Situ Recovery of Oil Shale. Draft Report, May. U.S. Bureau of Mines, Laramie, Wyoming.

232. Hartley, Fred L. 1958. Progress in Oil Shale Research, June. The Union Oil Co.

233. Reports. 1955–1959. Inspectors Reports. Colorado Bureau of Mines, Denver, Colorado.

234. Clampitt, R. L., *et al.* 1971. Gas Combustion Retorting Performance in a Large Demonstration Retort. Mobil Oil Company.

235. Staff. 1967. Project Bronco— PNE-1400. U.S. Atomic Energy Commission, Oct., Washington, D.C.

_____

Because the origins of many of these references are obscure, their presentation, here, does not always conform to standard style.

[Ed.]

Index